DOCUMENTS OF MODERN HISTORY

General Editors:

A. G. Dickens

Director, Institute of Historical Research, University of London

Alun Davies

Professor of Modern History, University College, Swansea

MARTIN LUTHER

edited by

E. G. Rupp

Dixie Professor of Ecclesiastical History,
University of Cambridge

and

Benjamin Drewery

Bishop Fraser Lecturer in Ecclesiastical History,
University of Manchester

New York · St. Martin's Press

© E. G. Rupp and Benjamin Drewery 1970

First published in
the United States of America in 1970
by St. Martin's Press, Inc,
175 Fifth Avenue, New York, New York

First published in Great Britain by
Edward Arnold (Publishers) Ltd

Library of Congress Catalog Card Number:
79-124955

Printed in Great Britain by
Robert Cunningham and Sons Ltd., Alva

CONTENTS

40842

PART V: FROM LUTHER TO LUTHERANISM, 1526–1535

PART VI: THE LAST DECADE

ABBREVIATIONS

W.A.	*Weimarer Ausgabe* (1883-)
W.A., Br.W.	*Weimarer Ausgabe, Briefwechsel*
W.A., T.R.	*Wiemarer Ausgabe, Tischreden*
Philad. Edn.	*Works of Martin Luther,* edited by H. E. Jacobs (Holman, and Castle Press, Philadelphia, 1931-2; Fortress Press, Philadelphia, 1943)
Amer. Edn.	*Luther's Works* (55 vols.) edited by J. Pelikan and H. J. Lehmann (Fortress Press, Philadelphia, 1943-)
Smith, *Life and Letters*	*The Life and Letters of Martin Luther,* edited by Preserved Smith (Murray, 1911)
Smith, *Correspondence*	*Luther's Correspondence and Other Contemporary Letters,* I, edited by Preserved Smith (Philadelphia, 1913)
Currie	*The Letters of Martin Luther,* edited by Margaret A. Currie (Macmillan, 1908)
Scheel	*Dokumente zu Luthers Entwicklung (bis 1519),* edited by Otto Scheel
Hillerbrand	*The Reformation in Its Own Words,* H. J. Hillerbrand (S.C.M. Press, 1964)
Kidd, *Doc.*	*Documents Illustrative of the Continental Reformation,* edited by B. J. Kidd (Oxford, 1911)
Rupp and Drewery	*De Servo Arbitrio* edited by E. G. Rupp *et al.,* Library of Christian Classics, XII (S.C.M. and Westminster Press, 1970)
Wace and Buchheim	*Luther's Primary Works,* edited by Henry Wace and Carl A. Buchheim (Murray, 1883)

Note: an asterisk (★) after the reference at the foot of a document indicates a translation by the present editors.

PREFACE

An English anthology of Luther has been long overdue. Captain Henry Bell's translation, in the seventeenth century, of the 'Table Talk' reminds us how splendid such a selection might have been in the full vigour of Elizabethan or Caroline prose, and how much of the blood has been drained away in the pernicious anaemia of modern 'historians' English'. It is in the letters that we catch the pathos, the humour, the humanity and genius of Luther and we have been glad to draw upon earlier selections from Margaret Currie and Preserved Smith. It was in the opening years of the Church struggle, 1517-21, that Luther himself counted most, for had he compromised or surrendered in those critical months whole ranges of history must have run in other directions. We have tried in a running commentary to link the various periods of his life with the progress of that enormous complexity, the Reformation itself. Luther was one who could say at the end of his life 'God has led me like an old, blind horse' and more than most men, as we shall see, he waited on events. We have tried to give documents as fully as possible, rather than innumerable extracts marred by too frequent running dots, which as all historians learn to fear often cover all manner of creeping things.

Two documents we have given complete: John Kessler's wonderful journalistic scoop, his account of 'How Martin Luther met me [!] on the way to Wittenberg', the unforgettable encounter of two students with the unknown knight on his way home from the Wartburg. And then, while all students know a little about the Bull *Exsurge Domine* in which Luther was condemned, few know the later Bull of excommunication, *Decet Romanum* (1521), equally fateful and much more illuminating about the meaning for Luther and his friends and patrons of his double condemnation by church and state. It proved hard to come by and we are grateful for the kindness of the Fathers of Heythrop College for the use of a copy found in the College Library. We have printed 'Eyn' Feste Burg' because no other hymn of the Reformation had such manifest impact on the souls of men; it stands apart with the 'Marseillaise' and the 'Battle Hymn of the Republic'. And not poor Miles

Coverdale nor dear Miss Winkworth come within a thousand miles
of Thomas Carlyle's translation, the one superb fragment of Luther to
be worthily translated. We hope this selection will encourage some to
press on, and to explore some of the wealth of material in the fifty-five
volumes of the modern American Lutheran edition of his writings.

Gordon Rupp
Benjamin Drewery

ACKNOWLEDGEMENTS

The publisher and editors gratefully acknowledge permission granted
by the following to reprint passages from copywright works: Fortress
Press, Philadelphia for extracts from *Luther's Works* (American Edition)
edited by Pelikan and Lehmann (E1, L5, N1, N6, N7, P1), and from
Works of Martin Luther (Philadelphia Edition) (M5, M6, M7, M8, M9,
M10, M11, M12, N4, O2, R6, V1); J. C. B. Mohr (Paul Siebeck),
Tübingen for extracts from *Dokumente zu Luthers Entwicklung* edited
by Otto Scheel (B5, V6,); S.C.M. Press, London, and Harper & Row,
New York for an extract from *The Reformation in Its Own Words* by
H. J. Hillerbrand (P2); and S.C.M. Press, London, and Westminster
Press, Philadelphia for an extract from *De Servo Arbitrio* translated and
edited by E. G. Rupp, P. S. Watson, A. N. Marlow and B. Drewery,
Vol. XIII, The Library of Christian Classics, 1970 (O6).

PART I *The Young Luther*

A   BIRTH, CHILDHOOD, EARLY LIFE

Martin Luther was born on St. Martin's day, 10 December 1483, at Eisleben, in Thuringian Saxony. His parents were Hans and Margaret Luther, and he had plenty of relatives in the neighbourhood of Möhra and Eisenach. In 1484 Hans Luther moved to the mining areas of Mansfeld and prospered enough to rent furnaces and to become a local councillor. Martin went to school, first at Mansfeld, then at Magdeburg and later at Eisenach, sharing the tough experiences of what was in a special sense, a 'beat generation'. In April 1501, 'Martinus Ludher ex Mansfeld' matriculated in the older University of Erfurt. Here he studied the Arts courses (B.A. 1501, M.A. 1505), learned to play the lute and talked enough to be nicknamed 'the philosopher'. Apart from the church, the law was the obvious profession for an ambitious and gifted young man, and Hans Luther intended his son to become a lawyer, paying for the necessary and expensive text books. He was infuriated to learn, in July 1505, that the son from whom he hoped so much had become a monk, and without consulting him, had entered the house of the Eremetical Order of St. Augustine, in Erfurt.

1-4   Fragments of Autobiography

I was born at Eisleben, and baptized in St. Peter's there. I do not remember this, but I believe my parents and fellow countrymen.

W.A., Br.W., I, 610.18*

2

I am the son of a peasant. My great-grandfather, grandfather and father were peasants. As he [Melanchthon] says, I might have become an overseer, bailiff, or some such village official, one servant among others with authority over the rest. Then my father moved to Mansfeld, where he became a miner. This is where I come from.

W.A., T.R., V, 6250*

3

From an inscription in a Bible, in Luther's hand, 1544.

To my dear old friend, Nicholas Omeler who carried me in his arms,
when I was little and weak, to and from school many a time.

W.A., XLVIII, 145.10*

4

On St. Alexis day, Luther said, 'To-day is the anniversary of my entering the monastery at Erfurt.' Then he began to tell the story of how he
had made his vow two weeks before when, travelling near Stottern-
heim, not far from Erfurt, he had been so shaken by a flash of lightning,
that he had cried out in terror, 'Help me, St. Anna, and I will become
a monk': 'but God took my vow in the fashion of Hebrew – Anna,
that is, under grace not the law! Afterwards I regretted the vow and
others tried to dissuade me. But I stuck to it, and on the day before
St. Alexis day I invited my best friends to a farewell, that they might
accompany me on the morrow. When they would have restrained me,
I said, "To-day you look on me for the last time." So, with tears, they
came with me. My father, too was angry about the vow, but I stuck to
my decision. I never dreamed of leaving the monastery. I had quite
died to the world.'

W.A., T.R., IV, 3707*

**5   Dedication to his Father of 'De Votis Monasticis
Iudicium,' 21 November 1521**

To Hans Luther, his father, Martin Luther, his son, sends greetings in
Christ.

In dedicating this book to you, dearest father, . . . I am taking the
opportunity, which this interchange between us conveniently provides,
of telling my pious readers the cause of the book, its argument, and the
example it offers.

    . . . It is now nearly sixteen years since I became a monk, against
your wishes and without your knowledge. In your paternal affection
you feared for my weakness, since I was then a youth, just entering my
twenty-second year, 'clothed in hot youth' (as Augustine says) [*Confessions* II, 3], and you had learned from many examples that this kind

of life has turned out badly for many. Your own plan for my future was to tie me down with an honourable and wealthy marriage. Your fears for me got on your mind and your anger against me was for a time implacable. . . . At last you gave it up and submitted your will to God, although your fears for me remained. For I remember only too well that after you were reconciled and talking with me again, I told you that I had been called by terrors from heaven and become a monk against my own will and desire (to say nothing of the inclinations of the flesh!) [*ventris gratia*]; I had been beleaguered by the terror and agony of sudden death, and I made my vows perforce and of necessity. Then you said – 'May it not prove an illusion and a deception.' That word penetrated and lodged in the depths of my soul, as if God had spoken through your mouth; but I hardened my heart against you and your word as much as I could. You said something else as well: when I presumed as your son to rebuke you for your anger, you suddenly lashed me with the retort – so fitting and so pointed that hardly any word spoken to me in my whole life has sounded more powerfully in my ears or lingered so long – 'Have you not also heard that parents are to be obeyed?' . . . For my vow was not worth a straw, because in taking it I was withdrawing myself from the will and authority of my parent.

WARTBURG

Latin in *W.A.*, VIII, 573 *et seq.**

B   LUTHER THE MONK

That Luther as a monk went through deep spiritual and theological anguish, is as well attested as anything in his life. At first all went well in the monastery, but when the busy novitiate was over, troubles began. He was troubled in conscience, and the many passages in his writings in which he speaks of the agony of a too scrupulous, bruised conscience reflect these experiences. Nor was he helped by the Nominalist theology dominant at Erfurt, which threw stress on the human will, but which had one or two devastating points of spiritual uncertainty. For Luther, theological and religious problems ran alongside and inside one another, and centred for him in the thought of the righteousness or justice of God (*Justitia Dei*).

1-4   Luther's Own Account of his Monastic Life

I was indeed a good monk and kept the rules of my order so strictly
that I can say: if ever a monk got to heaven through monasticism, I
should have been that man. All my brothers in the monastery who
know me will testify to this. I would have become a martyr through
fasting, prayer, reading and other good works had I remained a monk
very much longer.

W.A., XXXVIII, 143★

2

When I was a monk I tried with all diligence to live according to the
rule, and I used to be contrite, to confess and sedulously perform my
allotted penance. And yet my conscience could never give me certainty:
I always doubted and·said 'You did not do that correctly. You were
not contrite enough. You left that out of your confession.' The more
I tried to remedy an uncertain, weak and afflicted conscience with the
traditions of men, the more each day I found it more uncertain, weaker,
more troubled.

W.A., XL, 2.15.15★

3

Then remorse comes and terrifies the sinner. Then all's right with the
world and he alone is a sinner. God is gracious to the whole world,
save to him alone. Nobody has to meet the wrath of God save he alone;
he believes there is no wrath anywhere than that which he feels, and
he finds himself the most miserable of men. That is how it was with
Adam and Eve when they sinned. Had God not come in the cool of
the day they would never have noticed their sin. But when he came,
they crawled away. . . .

W.A., XIX, 210.14★

4

I knew a man, who said that he had suffered [the pains of eternal tor-
ments] in the shortest possible time, so great and infernal that 'nor
tongue nor pen can show' nor those believe who have not experienced
them, so that if they were to be completed, or lasted half an hour, or
even the tenth part of an hour, he would utterly perish and his bones
be reduced to ashes. Then God appears horrifyingly angry and with

him the whole creation. There can be no flight, nor consolation either from within or from without, but all is accusation.

W.A., I, 558.7*

5 Luther's 'Breakthrough' from the 'Autobiographical Fragment', March, 1545

That it was the 'justice of God' which focussed all Luther's trials and temptations can be attested from many levels of his writings – from his early lectures on *Psalms* and *Romans*, from his later sermons and commentaries, from his letters and his *Table Talk*. The one really extensive account of his spiritual pilgrimage at this point comes in the enigmatic *Autobiographical Fragment* which was appended to the 1545 edition of his works. This is on the whole an illuminating document. It shows that for Luther it was not only the 'justice of God' but the statement in *Romans* 1:17 that this 'justice' (understood as avenging and punishing) has been revealed by the Law *and* by the Gospel, which puzzled and tormented. He goes on to say with what mental relief and illumination he came to understand that 'justice' here means the gift of God by which men live by faith in God's forgiving mercy. There are however difficult problems when we try to pinpoint the date of this 'breakthrough', and historians and theologians continue and will continue to debate the matter. There are those (Vogelsang, Bornkamm and perhaps a majority of modern scholars) who suppose that it occurred during Luther's first course of lectures on the *Psalms* (1513-4) or at any rate before his lectures on *Romans* (1515-6), since it is difficult to see how he could have given this impressive and profound series, had he still been 'held up' (as he says) from entering the world of Pauline thought. Others (Bizer, Aland) stress that Luther's thought at this time is still within a Catholic framework, and would suggest that only at a later date, for example 1518, can we find in Luther a clearly evangelical, Protestant doctrine of faith in the promises of God, and an affirmation of salvation by faith alone rather than salvation by renunciation and humility. But it seems dangerous to read back into Luther's thought at this molten period, later classifications and clarifications, and we must not read too much of later Protestantism into his claims for his 'breakthrough', since he himself sees it clearly as not far removed from the doctrine of St. Augustine.

. . . Meanwhile, in that year [1519] I had once again turned to the task of interpreting the *Psalms*, relying on the fact that I was in better training for it since I had handled in the schools the epistles of St. Paul to the Romans and Galatians, and the epistle to the Hebrews. I had certainly been seized with a wondrous eagerness to understand Paul in the epistle to the Romans, but hitherto I had been held up – not by a 'lack of heat in my heart's blood',[1] but by one word only, in chapter 1: 'The

[1] Virgil, *Georgics*, ii.484.

righteousness [*justitia*] of God is revealed in [the Gospel].' For I hated this word 'righteousness of God', which by the customary use of all the doctors I had been taught to understand philosophically as what they call the *formal* or *active righteousness* whereby God is just and punishes unjust sinners.

For my case was this: however irreproachable my life as a monk, I felt myself in the presence of God [*coram Deo*] to be a sinner with a most unquiet conscience, nor could I believe him to be appeased by the satisfaction I could offer. I did not love – nay, I hated this just God who punishes sinners, and if not with silent blasphemy, at least with huge murmuring I was indignant against God, as if it were really not enough that miserable sinners, eternally ruined by original sin, should be crushed with every kind of calamity through the law of the Ten Commandments, but that God through the Gospel must add sorrow to sorrow, and even through the Gospel bring his righteousness and wrath to bear on us. And so I raged with a savage and confounded conscience; yet I knocked importunely at Paul in this place, with a parched and burning desire to know what he could mean.

At last, as I meditated day and night, God showed mercy and I turned my attention to the connection of the words, namely – 'The righteousness of God is revealed, as it is written: the righteous shall live by faith' – and there I began to understand that the righteousness of God is the righteousness in which a just man lives by the gift of God, in other words by faith, and that what Paul means is this: the righteousness of God, revealed in the Gospel, is *passive*, in other words that by which the merciful God justifies us through faith, as it is written, 'The righteous shall live by faith.' At this I felt myself straightway born afresh and to have entered through the open gates into paradise itself. There and then the whole face of scripture was changed; I ran through the scriptures as memory served, and collected the same analogy in other words, for example *opus Dei*, that which God works in us; *virtus Dei*, that by which God makes us strong; *sapientia Dei*, that by which He makes us wise; *fortitudo Dei, salus Dei, gloria Dei.*

And now, in the same degree as I had formerly hated the word 'righteousness of God', even so did I begin to love and extol it as the sweetest word of all; thus was this place in St. Paul to me the very gate of paradise. Later I read Augustine on the *Spirit and the Letter*, where beyond all hope I found that he also interprets the righteousness of God in the same way, as that in which God clothes us when he justifies us. And although Augustine's statement of this is still open to criticism, and he is neither clear nor comprehensive in the matter of imputation, yet he is satisfied that the righteousness of God should be taught to be that by which we are justified.

In the strengthened armour of such thoughts I began my second interpretation of the *Psalms*. . . .

I have told this story, gentle reader, that you may bear in mind, if you read my modest writings, that . . . I am one of those who (as Augustine said of himself) have improved as a writer and teacher, not of those who have suddenly from nothing become supreme, although they have done no works, undergone no temptations, had no experience, but with one glance at scripture exhausted the total spirit of its contents.[1]

Latin in Scheel, 191 *et seq.*★

C LUTHER'S PUBLIC AND ACADEMIC LIFE, 1509-15; THE THESES OF APRIL 1517

Whatever Luther's progress and his ups and downs, as a private person and as a monk he became more and more involved in public affairs. He was appointed a Prior and a District Vicar within his own order, a preacher first to his fellow monks, and then an official preacher in the parish church of Wittenberg, a popular audience which became of immense importance for him. He had been brought from Erfurt in 1509 to lecture in the Arts faculty at the new University of Wittenberg, where he now lectured on the *Nichomachean Ethics* of Aristotle. Sometime between 1510-12 he went to Rome on business connected with his order, and was affronted at the cynical professionalism of the clergy and the worldliness in high places. In 1512, encouraged by his teacher and friend, John Staupitz, he took his D.D., a status which involved defending sacred truth in public. On the retirement of Staupitz, Luther succeeded him as a Professor of Biblical Theology. He now became involved in a university ferment which was European-wide, the tension between an older scholasticism and the new humanism based on a return to 'the Bible and the Old Fathers'. This involved Luther in growing antagonism to his old teachers, especially the Nominalists at Erfurt. Alongside university lectures, which were apt to be dull, dictated affairs, the regular debates or disputations provided a useful ground for airing new and controversial opinions. In Wittenberg they took place on Fridays, week by week, and at the promotion of students to higher degrees, and

[1] The rest of this *Autobiographical Fragment* is translated at the end of this book (V.6).

on certain festal occasions. Over some of these Luther presided in those years when he was Dean, and one occasion in April 1517 gave rise to a formidable series of Ninety Seven Theses which were an all out attack on the schoolmen, and especially the Nominalist tradition of Gabriel Biel and of Luther's own teachers, Trutvetter and Usingen. Luther had by this time something of a reputation for controversy, and we know from his correspondence with his friend John Lang that he had seriously annoyed the Erfurt theologians. But when he sent them copies of the Ninety Seven Theses and offered to debate them, either in Wittenburg or in Erfurt, there was stony silence.

1   To John Braun, 17 March 1509

. . . I am now, by God's command or permission, settled in Wittenberg, and very well. Only the study of philosophy is most disagreeable to me, for from the first I would have preferred theology, that is, the theology which goes to the kernel of the nut and touches the bone and the flesh. . . .

MARTIN LUTHER
Augustinian
Currie, 3

WITTENBERG

2   To George Spenlein, Augustinian in Memmingen, 7 April 1516

. . . Beware, my brother, at aiming at a purity which rebels against being classed with sinners. For Christ only dwells among sinners. For this he came from heaven, where he dwelt among saints, so that he might also sojourn with the sinful. Strive after such love, and thou wilt experience his sweetest consolation. For if by our own efforts we are to attain peace of conscience, why then did Christ die? Therefore thou wilt only find peace in him when thou despairest of self and thine own works. He himself will teach thee how in receiving thee he makes thy sins his, and his righteousness thine. When thou believest this firmly (for he is damned who does not believe) then bear patiently with erring brothers, making their sins thine. . . .

Your Brother, MARTIN LUTHER
Augustinian
Currie, 4 *et seq.*

WITTENBERG

3   To John Lang, Prior at Erfurt, 26 October 1516

I would require two secretaries, for I do nothing almost all day but write letters, therefore if I repeat myself you will understand why it is.

I am lecturer in the cloister, reader at meals, preach daily, and direct the students' studies; I am the Prior's vicar (which means being vicar eleven times over), inspector of fish-ponds at Leitzkau, must espouse the Herzberg people's cause at Torgau, and be expounder of St. Paul and the *Psalms*, besides my letter-writing. Behold what a leisurely man I am, and in addition am plagued by the temptations of the world, the flesh, and the devil. . . .

I fear that with the plague here I shall not be able to continue. It has already robbed us of two or three, but not in one day. The smith opposite lost a son, who was in good health yesterday, and the other is infected. Yes, indeed, here it is, and is beginning to rage with great vehemence especially among the young. You counsel me to flee for refuge to you. But why?

The world will not come to an end although Brother Martin perish. But if the plague spread, I shall send the brothers out into the world. As for me, seeing I have been placed here, my vows of obedience demand that I remain till I am ordered elsewhere. Not that I have no fear of death, for I am not the Apostle Paul, but only his expounder, and I still hope the Lord will deliver me from this fear also.

Farewell, and think of us. Amen.

MARTIN LUTHER
Augustinian
Currie, 10 *et seq.*

WITTENBERG

4   To John Lang, 18 May 1517

Our theology and that of St. Augustine, by the grace of God, are making rapid progress in our university. Aristotle is continuing to fall from his throne, and his end is only a matter of time; and all object to hearing lectures on the text-books of the Sentences, and no one need expect an audience who does not expound this theology – that of the Bible or St. Augustine, or some other of the honoured Church teachers. Farewell, and pray for me.

WITTENBERG   MARTIN LUTHER

Currie, 15

5 To John Staupitz, 30 May 1518

I remember, reverend Father, among those happy and wholesome stories of yours, by which the Lord used wonderfully to console me, that you often mentioned the word 'penitence', whereupon, distressed by our consciences and by those torturers who with endless and intolerable precept taught nothing but what they called a method of confession, we received you as a messenger from heaven; for penitence is not genuine save when it begins from the love of justice and of God, and this which they consider the end and consummation of repentance is rather its commencement.

Your words on this subject pierced me like the sharp arrows of the mighty [*Psalms*, cxx: 4], so that I began to see what the scriptures had to say about penitence, and behold the happy result: the texts all supported and favoured your doctrine, in so much that, while there had formerly been no word in almost all the Bible more bitter to me than 'penitence' (although I zealously simulated it before God and tried to express an assumed and forced love), now no word sounds sweeter or more pleasant to me than that. For thus do the commands of God become sweet when we understand that they are not to be read in books only, but in the wounds of the sweetest Saviour.

After this it happened by the favour of the learned men who taught me Hebrew and Greek that I learned that the Greek word is μετάνοια from μετά and νοῦν, in other words, from 'afterwards' and 'mind', so that penitence or μετάνοια is 'coming to one's right mind, afterwards' [*Resipiscentia*], that is, comprehension of your own evil, after you had accepted loss and found out your error. This is impossible without a change in your affections. All this agrees so well with Paul's theology, that, in my opinion, at least, nothing is more characteristically Pauline.

Then I progressed and saw that μετάνοια meant not only 'afterwards' and 'mind', but also 'change' and 'mind', so that μετάνοια means change of mind and affection, and this seemed to suggest, not only the change of affection, but also the mode of the change, viz. the grace of God. . . .

Sticking fast to this conclusion, I dared to think that they were wrong who attributed so much to works of repentance that they have left us nothing of it but formal penances and elaborate confession. They were seduced by the Latin, for *poenitentiam agere* means rather a work than a change of affection and in no wise agrees with the Greek. . . .

Smith, Life and Letters, 91 et seq.

PART II *The Indulgence Controversy*

D   THE CONTROVERSY

The practice and theory of Papal Indulgences is an instance of the indefiniteness (*Unklarheit*) which the Catholic historian Lortz has defined as a hall-mark of the early sixteenth century. Recent discussion at the Second Vatican Council revealed how wide the range of debate about them is even in our own time. An Indulgence is a remission of temporal punishment due for sin, and has its origin in the medieval developments concerning the sacrament of penance, and the possibility of commuting the act of satisfaction demanded by the Church. In 1300 Pope Boniface VIII issued a Jubilee Indulgence, and so profitable did such devices become for a Papacy more and more financially embarrassed that these Jubilee Indulgences became more and more frequent. A theoretical justification for the practice was expounded by Alexander of Hales, in terms of the merits of Christ and the saints, and set out in the Bull *Unigenitus* (**D, 1**) of Clement VI, 1343, which included the statement that the Pope 'acquired a treasure for the Church militant'. In 1476 this was extended by Pope Sixtus IV (**D, 2**) to souls in purgatory. By the beginning of the sixteenth century Indulgences had become a *sacrum negotium* in the hands of the banking house of Fugger.

It was a Jubilee Indulgence issued by Pope Julius II in 1507 and renewed by Leo X in 1513 which sparked off the Reformation. The object, the rebuilding of St. Peter's – Rafael's and Michelangelo's St. Peter's! – was more worthy than some of the devices used to raise the money. Moreover by a secret agreement (of which most Germans, including Luther, were unaware) half of the proceeds from the sale in Germany were to go towards paying the huge debts of the young Archbishop Albert of Mainz, who was also Archbishop of Magdeburg, and administrator of the diocese of Halberstadt. The fees due to the Papacy amounted to something like 26,000 ducats and Albert had had to raise a further loan of 29,000 from the Fuggers. There was therefore an urgent financial pressure, which may be reflected in the terms of the Instructions for the Commissaries of Indulgences (**D, 3**) issued on Albert's orders, and the extravagant preaching of the Dominican John Tetzel.

Debate about Indulgences was no new thing and had been discussed by moralists often enough. In Wittenberg, Martin Luther had attacked Indulgences in sermons, in 1515 and 1516, and put himself in some disfavour with the Saxon court, since there were important Indulgences connected with the enormous collection of holy relics which the Elector Frederick the Wise housed in the Collegiate Church of All Saints, Wittenberg. Luther then wrote a letter to Albert of Mainz (**D, 4**), complaining especially about the Instructions to the Commissaries and asking that they be withdrawn: in a postscript he asked Albert to glance at the enclosed theses (**D, 5**), from which he would see how uncertain and dubious was the whole practice. Luther may also have written to his own Ordinary, the Bishop of Brandenburg. It is likely that he had already nailed a copy of the Theses, in placard form, on the door of All Saints Church, in the normal way of University disputations, and he may have given copies to his nearest academic colleagues. The original copies of the Theses have not survived, and we do not know how many were written by hand, or whether a first batch was run off by the University printer. No public disputation ever took place on them in Wittenberg. When copies of these Latin Theses were translated into German and when they got in the hands of the printers, they circulated swiftly throughout Germany, rousing a furore in all quarters. The counter-theses of Tetzel and Wimpina only added fuel to the controversy, and Luther found himself in the centre of a growing and dangerous public affair. Moreover, as his lawyer friend, Schürpf had warned him, the Theses touched matters far more delicate and dangerous than Indulgences, for they called in question the Papal 'plenitude of power', and it was this implicit and hardly-recognized challenge to Papal authority which led to the widening and deepening of the struggle until it became the most formidable schism in the history of the western Church.

In 1517 the promulgation in Germany of the Jubilee Indulgences was on a much bigger scale than the Wittenberg relics with their falling revenue. Luther, on 31 October, the vigil of All Saints, may well have felt that something more striking was needed than his protest in the pulpit on that day, a year before. The Saxon authorities had indeed forbidden the sale of the Jubilee Indulgences in their territory, intending to keep currency within their own borders, but it was easy enough for Saxons to get across the frontier, and to return with certificates and with stories offensive to Luther's pious ears. Luther now wrote the Ninety-five Theses about the theology and the scope of Indulgences. He seems to have enjoyed writing Theses, as he certainly enjoyed debates, and these may have seemed much milder than the onslaught on scholastic theology (the Ninety-seven Theses) which he had written six months earlier. Some of the things he wrote were tentative, some exaggerated purposely for the use of debate. They seemed to be a protest by a theologian against a practical abuse. An analysis of them in the light of Luther's letters, lectures and writings before and after their publication shows in them the marks of his 'Theology of the Cross' (**E**), and his debt to German mysticism and to his own Biblical studies.

(There are good factual accounts of Indulgences, and of the events which began 31 October 1517, in all the textbooks, especially J. M. Todd, *M. Luther*, London, 1964, Appendix I. For the view that Luther did not nail the Theses, since he would not have wished to make a public scene while, in the light of his letter to Albert of Mainz, they were still *sub judice*, see Erwin Iserloh, *The Theses were not Posted*, London, 1968. But although Iserloh's account of Indulgences and of events in Germany is excellent he has his own theological reasons for denying the event, and his handling of the evidence leaves something to be desired. See *Journal of Theological Studies*, XIX (1), 1968, 360 *et seq.* for a critical review in English by E. G. Rupp and references to the large German literature which has sprung up. On the theology of the Ninety-five Theses see Rupp, 'Luther's Ninety-five Theses and the Theology of the Cross' in *Luther for an Ecumenical Age*, edited by C. S. Meyer, St. Louis, 1967, 67 *et seq.*)

1   The Theory of Indulgences: from the Bull 'Unigenitus' of Pope Clement VI, 27 January 1343

The only-begotten Son of God deigned to come down from his Father's bosom into the womb of his mother, in whom and from whom he joined, by an ineffable union, the substance of our mortality to his divinity, in unity of Person. . . . His purpose was in this way to redeem fallen humanity and make satisfaction for him to God the Father. . . . Nor did he redeem us with corruptible things – with silver and gold – but with his own precious blood, which he is known to have poured out as an innocent victim on the altar of the cross: not a mere measured drop of blood (which however because of its union with the Word would have sufficed for the redemption of all humanity) but as it were an unmeasured flood. . . . What a great treasure, then, did the holy Father acquire therefrom for the church militant, lest the mercy of so great an outpouring be made empty, useless or superfluous! . . . those who avail themselves of this infinite treasure are given a share in God's friendship [*Wisdom*, VIII: 14].

Now this treasure he entrusted to be dispensed for the weal of the faithful . . . through blessed Peter, who bore the keys of heaven, and Peter's successors as God's own representatives on earth. The purposes served should be proper and reasonable: sometimes total, sometimes partial remission of punishment due for temporal sins, as well generally as specially (according as they learn it to be expedient with God); and for these ends the treasure should be applied in mercy to those who are truly penitent and have made their confession.

The mass of this treasure is known to have been increased by the merits of the blessed mother of God and of all the elect, from the first

righteous man to the last. Nor is there any fear of its being used up or
diminished, as well because of the infinite merits of Christ ... as because the greater the number who are drawn to righteousness by its
application, the greater grows the mass of merits themselves. ...

Latin in Kidd, Doc. 1*

2   The First Application of Indulgences to Souls in Purgatory: from the Bull 'Salvator Noster' of Pope Sixtus IV, 3 August 1476

... Our aim is that the salvation of souls may be secured above all at
that time when they most need the intercessions of others and are least
able to help themselves. We wish by our Apostolic authority to draw
on the treasury of the Church and to succour the souls in purgatory
who died united with Christ through love and whose lives have merited
that such intercessions should now be offered through an Indulgence of
this kind.

With the longings of such great paternal affection as with God's help
we can achieve, in reliance on the divine mercy and the plenitude of
our power, we grant by concession and indulgence as follows:

If any parents, friends or other Christians are moved by obligations
of piety towards these very souls who are exposed to the fire of purgatory for the expiation of punishments which by divine justice are
their due:

let them during the stated period of ten years give a fixed amount
or value of money, as laid down by its dean and chapter or by our
own collector, for the repair of the church of Saints, paying either in
person at the Church or by duly accredited messengers:

it is then our will that plenary remission should avail by intercession for the said souls in purgatory, to win them relief from their
punishments – the souls, that is, for whose sakes the stated quantity
or value of money has been paid in the manner declared. ...

Latin in Kidd, Doc. 2*

3   The 'Instructio Summaria' of Albert of Mainz

From the end of 1514 Pope Leo X began to issue commissions of Indulgences
to German and neighbouring provinces; the third was to Albert, Elector Arch-

bishop of Mainz, 31 March 1515, for his provinces of Mainz and Magdeburg. Albert issued the following *Instructio* to his sub-commissaries:

. . . The following are the four principal gifts of grace that have been granted by the Apostolic Bull: any one of them can be had separately. It is on these four Indulgences that the preachers must concentrate their utmost diligence, infiltrating them one by one into the ears of the faithful in the most effective way, and explaining them with all the ability they have.

The first principal grace is the plenary remission of all sins – the greatest of all graces, for the reason that man, a sinner who is deprived of divine grace, obtains through it perfect remission and God's grace anew. In addition, through this remission of sins, punishments to be undergone in purgatory because of offence done to the divine majesty, are remitted in full, and the punishments of the said purgatory are totally wiped out. Now it is true that no possible repayment could be sufficient to earn so great a grace, for the reason that God's gift and his grace are beyond valuation; nevertheless, that the invitation of Christians to secure it may be made easier, we lay down the following procedure:

First, let every penitent who has made oral confession visit at least seven of the churches appointed for this purpose – that is, those in which the Papal arms are installed – and in each church let him say with devotion five Paternosters and five Ave Marias, to render honour to the five wounds of our Lord Jesus Christ, through whom has been enacted our redemption. . . .

For those who are confined to their beds there may be deputed a dedicated image before which or to which they may say certain prayers according to the ruling of the penitentiary. . . .

If anyone for any reason seeks to be excused the visit to the said churches or altars, the penitentiaries, having heard the reason, may allow it: such a visit may be compounded by a larger financial contribution.

This money must be placed in a box. But the contributions for the repository in aid of the construction of the building of the Chief of the Apostles will be sought as follows: first the penitentiaries and confessors, after expounding the magnitude of such plenary remission and Indulgences to those who confess, will ask them how much in money or other temporal possessions their consciences tell them it is worth to make good the lack of such plenary remission and Indulgences; they will ask this to facilitate their subsequent inducements to contribute. And since human conditions vary far too much for us to take separate account of them all and lay an appropriate assessment on each, we classify them in general terms and assess the classes as follows. . . . [*Albert then assesses at fixed amounts all classes from kings and archbishops down through abbots and barons to priests and merchants and the lesser orders of society concluding with*] the penniless, who may make good their contribution by prayers and fasting: for the kingdom of Heaven should not stand open for the rich more than for the poor. . . .

The second principal grace is the confessional, carrying with it the greatest, most relevant and previously unknown Indulgences. . . . Its contents and their significance the preachers and confessors must explain and extol with all their power. In the confessional the following concessions are made for those who pay for it:

1   The right to choose as a suitable confessor even a regular of a mendicant order who can in the first place absolve them from having to seek a settlement of complaints that other men can bring against them.

2   He can absolve them once in the course of their lives and also *in articulo mortis* from certain of the gravest sins, even those which are reserved for the Apostolic See.

3   He can absolve them from cases not reserved for the Apostolic See as often as is necessary.

4   He can apply plenary Indulgence of all sins since in the course of the confessor's life and *in articulo mortis* as often as death threatens, even if the threat does not materialize.

5   He can commute any kind of vows for other works of piety, except solemn vows undertaken overseas or of a pilgrimage to the thresholds of the Apostles (and of St. James in Compostela) or of the religious life and of chastity.

6   He can administer the sacrament of the Eucharist at any time of the year except on Easter day and *in articulo mortis*.

We order that one of these confessionals must be made generally available to ensure that the poor are not excluded from the graces it contains, . . . the reckoning being a quarter of a golden Rhenish florin which (quite apart from the usual assessment) must be placed in the Indulgence-repository. . . .

The third principal grace is participation in all the blessings of the universal Church. . . .

The fourth principal grace is the plenary remission of all sins for the souls that exist in purgatory, which the Pope grants and concedes by means of intercessions, so that a contribution placed by the living in the repository on their behalf counts as one which a man might make or give for himself. . . . There is no need for the contributors to be of contrite heart or to make oral confession, since this grace depends (as the Bull makes clear) on the love in which the departed died and the contributions which the living pay. . . .

Latin in Kidd, Doc. 6*

4   To Albert of Mainz, 31 October 1517

To the Right Reverend Father in Christ, Lord Albrecht, Archbishop of Magdeburg and Mainz, Margrave of Brandenburg, his esteemed lord and shepherd in Christ. The grace of God be with him.

May your Electoral Highness graciously permit me, the least and most unworthy of men, to address you. The Lord Jesus is my witness that I have long hesitated, on account of my unworthiness, to carry out what I now boldly do, moved thereto by a sense of the duty I owe you, Right Reverend Father. May your Grace look graciously on me, dust and ashes, and respond to my longing for your ecclesiastical approval.

With your Electoral Highness's consent, the Papal Indulgence for the rebuilding of St. Peter's in Rome is being carried through the land. I do not complain so much of the loud cry of the preacher of Indulgences, which I have not heard, but regret the false meaning which the simple folk attach to it, the poor souls believing that when they have purchased such letters they have secured their salvation, also, that the moment the money jingles in the box souls are delivered from purgatory, and that all sins will be forgiven through a letter of Indulgence, even that of reviling the blessed mother of God, were any one blasphemous enough to do so. And, lastly, that through these Indulgences the man is freed from all penalties! Ah, dear God! Thus are those souls which have been committed to your care, dear Father, being led in the paths of death, and for them you will be required to render an account. For the merits of no bishop can secure the salvation of the souls entrusted to him which is not always assured through the grace of God, the Apostle admonishing us 'to work out our own salvation with fear and trembling', and that the way which leads to life is so narrow, that the Lord, through the prophets Amos and Zechariah, likens those who attain to eternal life to brands plucked from the burning, and above all, the Lord points to the difficulty of redemption. Therefore, I could be silent no longer.

How then can you, through false promises of Indulgences, which do not promote the salvation or sanctification of their souls, lead the people into carnal security, by declaring them free from the painful consequences of their wrong-doing with which the Church was wont to punish their sins?

For deeds of piety and love are infinitely better than Indulgences, and yet the bishops do not preach these so earnestly, although it is their principal duty to proclaim the love of Christ to their people. Christ has nowhere commanded Indulgences to be preached, only the Gospel. So to what danger does a bishop expose himself, who instead of having the Gospel proclaimed among the people, dooms it to silence, while the cry of Indulgences resounds through the land? Will Christ not say to them, 'Ye strained at a gnat, and swallowed a camel'?

In addition, Reverend Father, it has gone abroad under your name, but doubtless without your knowledge, that this Indulgence is the priceless gift of God, whereby the man may be reconciled to God, and escape the fires of purgatory, and that those who purchase the Indulgences have no need of repentance.

What else can I do, Right Reverend Father, than beg your Serene Highness, carefully to look into this matter, and do away with this little book of instructions, and command those preachers to adopt another style of preaching, else another may arise and refute them, by writing another book in answer to the previous one, to the confusion of your Serene Highness, the very idea of which alarms me greatly. I hope that your Serene Highness may graciously deign to accept the faithful service which your insignificant servant, with true devotion, would render you. The Lord keep you to all eternity. Amen.

WITTENBERG, *the night before All Saints' Day 1517*

If agreeable to your Grace, perhaps you would glance at my enclosed theses, that you may see the opinion on the Indulgences is a very varied one, while those who proclaim them fancy they cannot be disputed. Your unworthy son,

MARTIN LUTHER
Augustinian, set apart as Doctor of Sacred Theology
Currie, 17 *et seq.*

5   The Ninety-five Theses, October 1517

1   When our Lord and Master, Jesus Christ, said 'Repent . . .', he meant that the whole life of believers should be one of penitence.

2   The word cannot be understood as referring to the sacrament of penance, in other words of confession and satisfaction, as administered by priests.

3   Yet he did not restrict it to inward penitence only; for inward penitence is nothing unless it produces outwardly the various mortifications of the flesh.

4   Hence as long as hatred of self remains (i.e. true inward penitence) the penalty of sin remains, that is, until we enter the kingdom of heaven.

5   The Pope has neither the will nor the power to remit any penalties beyond those he has imposed either at his own discretion or by canon law.

6   The Pope can remit no guilt, but only declare and confirm that it has been remitted by God; or, at most, he can remit it in cases reserved to his discretion. To ignore such remissions would of course leave the guilt untouched.

7   God never remits guilt to anyone without, at the same time, humbling him in total submission to the priest, his representative.

8   The penitential canons apply only to the living, and, according to the canons themselves, none applies to the dying.

9   Accordingly, the Holy Spirit does well for us through the Pope, by always making exception in his decrees of cases of imminent death or necessity.

10   It is ignorant and wrong for priests to reserve for the dying the canonical penalties in purgatory.

11   When canonical penalties were changed into penance in purgatory, the bishops must have been asleep while tares were being sown.

12   In former days, canonical penalties were imposed not after but before absolution, as evidence of true contrition.

13   The dying will pay all their debts by their death; and they are already dead to the canon laws and free from their jurisdiction.

14   Defective spiritual health or love in a dying man must needs bring with it a great fear, and the greater the deficiency the greater the fear.

15   This fear and horror is sufficient in itself (to pass over all else) to constitute the penalty of purgatory, since it comes very near the horror of despair.

16   There seems to be the same difference between hell, purgatory, and heaven as between despair, near despair, and assurance.

17   It seems that for souls in purgatory their love is necessarily increased as their horrors are abated.

18   Nor does it seem proved, on any grounds of reason or scripture, that those souls are outside the state of merit, or unable to grow in love.

19   Nor does it seem proved that they – or at least all of them – are certain and assured of their salvation, even if we are very certain of it ourselves.

20   Therefore the Pope, by his plenary remission of all penalties, does not mean 'all' in the absolute sense, but only those imposed by himself.

21   Hence those preachers of Indulgences are wrong when they say that a man is absolved and saved from every penalty by the Pope's Indulgences.

22   Rather, he cannot remit to souls in purgatory any penalty which canon law declares should have been paid in this present life.

23   If any remission of all penalties whatsoever can be granted to anyone, it can only be to those who are most perfect, in other words to very few.

24   It must therefore follow that the greater part of the people are deceived by that indiscriminate and high-sounding promise of freedom from penalty.

25   The same power as the Pope has in general over purgatory is possessed in particular by every single bishop in his bishopric and curate in his parish.

26   The Pope does excellently when he grants remission to the souls – not by the power of the keys (for he has none), but through intercession.

27   It is mere human talk to preach that the soul flies out [of purgatory] immediately the money clinks in the collection-box.

28   It is certainly possible that when the money clinks in the collection-box greed and avarice can increase; but the intercession of the Church depends on the will of God alone.

29   Who knows if all the souls in purgatory wish to be redeemed in view of the story told of St. Severinus and Paschal?[1]

30   No one is sure of the reality of his own contrition, much less of receiving plenary forgiveness.

---

[1] Seventh- and ninth-century Popes, who (according to legend) were themselves willing to forgo the beatific vision they had inherited and to suffer the pains of purgatory for the benefit of the faithful.

31   A man who truly buys Indulgences is as rare as a true penitent, in other words very rare indeed.

32   All those who believe themselves certain of their own salvation because of letters of pardon, will be eternally damned, together with their teachers.

33   We must especially beware of those who say that the Papal pardons are that inestimable divine gift by which a man is reconciled to God.

34   For the gifts of grace conveyed by these pardons relate only to the penalties of sacramental satisfaction which have been decreed by man.

35   It is not Christian preaching to teach that those who aim to redeem their souls, or to purchase confessional Indulgences, have no need of contrition.

36   Any Christian whatsoever who is truly repentant has, as his due, plenary remission from penalty and guilt, even without letters of Indulgence.

37   Any true Christian whatsoever, living or dead, participates in all benefits of Christ and the Church; and this is granted him by God, even without letters of Indulgence.

38   Yet the Pope's remission and dispensation are in no way to be despised, for, as already said, they proclaim the divine remission.

39   It is very difficult, even for the most learned theologians, to extol to the people at the same time the bounty of Indulgences and the need for true contrition.

40   True contrition seeks out and loves to pay the penalties of sin; whereas the bounty of Indulgences relaxes the penalties and makes men resent them – or at least it *can* do.

41   Apostolic pardons should only be preached with caution, lest people wrongly understand that they are more important than other good works of love.

42   Christians should be taught that the Pope has no thought that the purchase of Indulgences should be understood as at all comparable with works of mercy.

43   Christians should be taught that one who gives to the poor, or lends to the needy, does a better action than if he purchases pardons.

44   This is because, by a work of love, love grows and a man becomes better; whereas, by pardons, he does not become better, but only more free from punishment.

45   Christians should be taught that he who sees a needy person and passes him by, although he gives money for pardons, wins for himself not Papal Indulgences but the wrath of God.

B

46   Christians should be taught that, unless they abound in possessions beyond their needs, their duty is to retain what is necessary for their own household, and in no way to squander it in buying pardons.

47   Christians should be taught that the purchase of pardons is voluntary not obligatory.

48   Christians should be taught that, in granting pardons, the Pope has more need, and more desire, for devout prayer on his own behalf than for ready money.

49   Christians should be taught that the Pope's pardons are useful only if they do not rely on them, but most harmful if they lose the fear of God through them.

50   Christians should be taught that, if the Pope knew the exactions of the preachers of Indulgences, he would rather have the basilica of St. Peter reduced to ashes than built with the skin, flesh and bones of his sheep.

51   Christians should be taught that the Pope would be willing, as he ought if necessity should arise, to sell the church of St. Peter, and give of his own money to the great number from whom certain pardon-merchants are extorting it.

52   It is vain to rely on salvation through letters of pardon, even if the commissary, or indeed the Pope himself, were to put his own soul in pledge for them.

53   It is the enemies of Christ and of the Pope who forbid the word of God to be preached at all in some churches, in order that pardons may be preached in others.

54   The Word of God suffers injury if, in the same sermon, an equal or longer time is devoted to pardons than to that Word.

55   The mind of the Pope must necessarily be that if pardons (a very small matter) are celebrated by a single bell, by single processions and ceremonies, the Gospel (a very great matter) should be preached to the accompaniment of a hundred bells, a hundred processions, a hundred ceremonies.

56   The treasures of the Church, out of which the Pope gives Indulgences, are not sufficiently spoken of or known among the people of Christ.

57   It is at least clear that they are not temporal from the fact that many of the merchants do not scatter them freely, but only collect them.

58   Nor are they the merits of Christ and the saints, because, quite apart from the Pope, these merits are always working grace in the inner man, and cross, death and hell in the outer man.

59   St. Laurence said that the poor were the treasures of the Church, but in saying this he was using the language of his own time.

60   We do not speak rashly in saying that the keys of the Church are its treasure, and are bestowed by the merits of Christ.

61   For it is clear that the power of the Pope suffices, by itself, for the remission of penalties and (reserved) cases.

62   The true treasure of the Church is the holy Gospel of the glory and the grace of God.

63   But this is deservedly the most hated, for it makes the first to be the last.

64   On the other hand, the treasure of Indulgences is deservedly most popular, for it makes the last to be the first.

65   Therefore the treasures of the Gospel are nets which, in former times, they used to fish for men of wealth.

66   The treasures of the Indulgences are the nets which they use to fish for men of wealth today.

67   The Indulgences, which the merchants extol as the greatest gifts of grace, are rightly understood as 'greatest' only as far as money-getting is concerned.

68   But they are in truth least of all comparable with the grace of God and the piety of the cross.

69   Bishops and curates are in duty bound to receive the commissaries of the Apostolic pardons with all reverence.

70   But they are under a much greater obligation to give all their eyes and ears to prevent these men preaching their own dreams instead of the Pope's commission.

71   Let him be anathema and accursed who denies the truth of the Apostolic pardons.

72   On the other hand, let him be blessed who is on his guard against the wantonness and licence of the pardon-merchants' words.

73   Just as the Pope rightly thunders against those who contrive by any means to make a fraud of the business of pardons.

74   Much more does he intend to thunder against those who use the pretext of Indulgences to make a fraud of holy love and truth.

75   It is madness to think that Papal pardons have so much power that they can absolve a man even if he has done the impossible and violated the mother of God.

76   We assert the contrary, that the Pope's pardons are not able to remove the least of venial sins as far as their guilt is concerned.

77   When it is said that not even St. Peter, if he were now Pope, could

bestow greater gifts of grace, it is blasphemy against St. Peter and the Pope.

78 We assert the contrary, that both he and any Pope whatever, possesses greater gifts of grace – the Gospel, virtues, graces of healing, etc., as in *I Corinthians* XII.

79 It is blasphemy to say that the cross erected with the insignia of the Papal arms is of equal value with the cross of Christ.

80 Bishops, curates, and theologians who authorize such preaching to the people, will have to answer for it.

81 This wanton preaching of pardons makes if difficult even for learned men to redeem respect due to the Pope from the slanders or at least the shrewd questionings of the laity.

82 For example: 'Why does not the Pope empty purgatory for the sake of most holy love and the supreme need of souls? This would be the most righteous of reasons, if he can redeem innumerable souls for sordid money with which to build a basilica, the most trivial of reasons.'

83 Again: 'Why should requiems and anniversary masses for the dead continue to be said? And why does not the Pope repay, or permit to be repaid, the benefactions instituted for the dead, since it is wrong to pray for those souls who are now redeemed?'

84 Again: 'Surely this is a new sort of piety, on the part of God and the Pope, when they allow an impious man, an enemy of God, to pay money to redeem a devout soul, a friend of God; while yet they do not redeem, for free love's sake, the pious and beloved soul without payment, on account of its own need?'

85 Again: 'Whereas the penitential canon laws, which in fact and through disuse, have long been repealed and dead in themselves, why are dispensations from them still bought for money, through the granting of Indulgences, as if they were fully operative?'

86 Again: 'Since the Pope's wealth is larger than that of the crassest Crassi of our time, why does he not build this one basilica of St. Peter with his own money, rather than with that of the faithful poor?'

87 Again: 'What does the Pope remit or dispense to people who, by their perfect contrition, have a right to plenary remission and dispensation?'

88 Again: 'What greater good would be done to the Church if the Pope were to bestow these remissions and dispensations, not once, as now, but a hundred times a day, on any believer whatever.'

89 'Since the Pope seeks by Indulgences not money so much as the salvation of souls, why does he suspend the letters and pardons for-

merly conceded, as they are still as efficacious as they ever were?'
90   To suppress these most conscientious questionings of the laity by
authority only, instead of refuting them by reason, is to expose the
Church and the Pope to the ridicule of their enemies, and to make
Christian people unhappy.
91   If, therefore, pardons were preached in accordance with the spirit
and mind of the Pope, all these difficulties would be easily overcome,
or rather would never have arisen.
92   Away, then, with those prophets who say to Christ's people,
'Peace, peace!' when there is no peace.
93   Good riddance to all of those prophets who say to Christ's people,
'The cross, the cross!' when there is no cross.
94   Christians should be exhorted to seek earnestly to follow Christ,
their Head, through penalties, deaths, and hells.
95   And let them thus be more confident of entering heaven through
many tribulations rather than through a false assurance of peace.

Latin in Kidd, Doc. 11*

6   To Christopher Scheurl, 5 March 1517

To the learned Herr Christopher Scheurl, my esteemed friend in Christ,
my greeting! I have received two letters from you, a Latin and a
German one, my good Christopher, along with a present from that outstanding man, Albrecht Dürer, and my Latin and German propositions.
You wonder I did not tell you of them. But I did not wish to have them
widely circulated. I only intended submitting them to a few learned
men for examination, and if they disapproved of them, to suppress
them; or make them known through their publications, in the event
of their meeting with their approval. But now they are being spread
abroad and translated everywhere, which I never could have credited,
so that I regret having given birth to them – not that I am unwilling to
proclaim the truth manfully, for there is nothing I more ardently
desire, but because this way of instructing the people is of little avail.
As yet I am still uncertain as to some points, and would have gone into
others more particularly, leaving some out entirely, had I foreseen all
this.

From the rapid spread of the theses I gather what the greater part of
the nation think of this kind of Indulgence, in spite of them having to
disguise their opinions for fear of the Jews; still I must have the proofs
of my propositions in readiness, although I cannot publish them yet,

having been delayed through the Bishop of Brandenburg – whose advice I asked – being so long in returning them. Yes, when the Lord grants me leisure, I propose issuing a book on the use and misuse of the Indulgences, in order to suppress the before-mentioned points. I have no longer any doubt that the people are deceived, not through the Indulgences, but through their use. When I have finished these pro-positions I will send them to you. . . . Meantime, pray remember me to Albrecht Dürer that excellent man, and assure him of my continued gratitude. . . .

WITTENBERG   MARTIN LUTHER

Currie, 22 *et seq.*

7   To John Sylvius Egranus at Zwickau, 24 March 1518

. . . A man of signal and talented learning and of learned talent, has recently written a book called *Obelisks* against my theses. I mean John Eck, Doctor of Theology, Chancellor of the University of Ingolstadt, Canon of Eichstätt, and now, at length, Preacher at Augsburg, a man already famous and widely known by his books. What cuts me most is that we had recently formed a great friendship. Did I not already know the machinations of Satan, I should be astonished at the fury with which Eck has broken that sweet amity without warning and with no letter to bid me farewell.

In his *Obelisks* he calls me a fanatic Hussite, heretical, seditious, in-solent and rash, not to speak of such slight abuse as that I am dreaming, clumsy, unlearned, and that I despise the Pope. In short, the book is nothing but the foulest abuse, expressly mentioning my name and directed against my Theses. It is nothing less than the malice and envy of a maniac. I would have swallowed this sop for Cerberus, but my friends compelled me to answer it. Blessed be the Lord Jesus, and may he alone be glorified while we are confounded for our sins. Rejoice, brother, rejoice, and be not terrified by these whirling leaves, nor stop teaching as you have begun, but rather be like the palm tree which grows better when weights are hung on it. . . .

MARTIN LUTHER

WITTENBERG   *Augustinian*

Smith, *Correspondence*, I, 76 *et seq.*

E THE 'THEOLOGY OF THE CROSS'

Though Luther's 'Theology of the Cross' is something which he never repudiated or outgrew, it represents certain theological stresses which are particularly prominent in the period immediately before and after the opening of the Indulgence controversy. Its origin is in part to be found in the 'inward religion' of the German mystics, and especially in the writings of the Strasbourg Dominican John Tauler and in the little German tract, Luther's first publication, which we know as the *Theologia Germanica*. But it owes much also to Luther's own studies in Augustine and in the Bible. The cross of Christ is not simply something which Jesus Christ endured, but it is something which all his followers are called to share, as a life-long penitence, and as their 'old man' is daily crucified with its lusts and creaturely, egocentric desires. Luther uses a text from *Isaiah* (xxviii: 21) which speaks about God using a 'Strange Work', as the basis of a distinction between God's or Christ's 'Strange Work' and 'His Own (*proprium*) Work'. The 'Strange Work' is that by which sin is condemned in our own conscience: we are brought by its accusation into awareness of our own guilt before God, and to despair of our own righteousness or ability to save ourselves. The one is the work of Christ's cross, the other of his resurrection. There is here the beginning of Luther's important distinction between law and Gospel, which he develops in the following years. In addition, Luther's 'Theology of the Cross' stands in contrast to the scholastic doctrine of speculation about God's attributes, what Luther calls a 'Theology of Glory'. It is in the crucified Jesus that we behold God, in a divine folly and weakness which is stronger and wiser than men (Luther's thought at this point keeps close to the Pauline Christology of *I Corinthians*). (An excellent introduction to Luther's 'Theology of the Cross' will be found in P. S. Watson, *Let God be God*, London, 1947, Chapter 4.)

1 The Heidelberg Disputation, April 1518: Extracts from the 'Theses' and their 'Proofs'

13
Free will, after the fall, exists in name only, and as long as it does what it is able to do, it commits a mortal sin. . . .

14
Free will, after the fall, has power to do good only in a passive capacity, but it can always do evil in an active capacity. . . .

16

*The person who believes that he can obtain grace by doing what is in him
adds sin to sin so that he becomes doubly guilty. . . .*

17

*Nor does speaking in this manner give cause for despair, but for arousing the
desire to humble oneself and seek the grace of Christ. . . .*

19

*That person does not deserve to be called a theologian who looks upon the
invisible things of God as though they were clearly perceptible in those things
which have actually happened. . . .*

20

*He deserves to be called a theologian, however, who comprehends the visible
and manifest things of God seen through suffering and the cross.*

The manifest and visible things of God are placed in opposition to the
invisible, namely, his human nature, weakness, foolishness. The Apostle
in *I Corinthians* I [:25] calls them the weakness and folly of God. Because men misused the knowledge of God through works, God wished
again to be recognized in suffering, and to condemn wisdom concerning invisible things by means of wisdom concerning visible things, so
that those who did not honour God as manifested in his works should
honour him as he is hidden in his suffering. As the Apostle says in
I Corinthians I [:21], 'For since, in the wisdom of God, the world did
not know God through wisdom, it pleased God through the folly of
what we preach to save those who believe.' Now it is not sufficient for
anyone, and it does him no good to recognize God in his glory and
majesty, unless he recognizes him in the humility and shame of the
cross. Thus God destroys the wisdom of the wise, as *Isaiah* [XLV:15]
says, 'Truly, thou art a God who hidest thyself.'

So, also, in *John* XIV [:8], where Philip spoke according to the theology of glory: 'Show us the Father.' Christ forthwith set aside his flighty
thought about seeing God elsewhere and led him to himself, saying,
'Philip, he who has seen me has seen the Father' [John XIV:9]. For this
reason true theology and recognition of God are in the crucified Christ,
as it is also stated in *John* X [*John* XIV:6]: 'No one comes to the Father,
but by me.' 'I am the door' [*John* X:9], and so forth.

21

*A theology of glory calls evil good and good evil. A theology of the cross calls
the thing what it actually is. . . .*

22

That wisdom which sees the invisible things of God in works as perceived by man is completely puffed up, blinded, and hardened. . . .

23

The law brings the wrath of God, kills, reviles, accuses, judges and condemns everything that is not in Christ. . . .

24

Yet that wisdom is not of itself evil, nor is the law to be evaded: but without the theology of the cross man misuses the best in the worst manner. . . .

26

The law says 'Do this' and it is never done. Grace says 'Believe this' and everything is already done. . . .

28

The love of God does not find, but creates, that which is pleasing to it. The love of man comes into being through that which is pleasing to it.

The second part is clear and is accepted by all philosophers and theologians, for the object of love is its cause, assuming, according to Aristotle, that all power of the soul is passive, and material and active only in receiving something. Thus it is also demonstrated that Aristotle's philosophy is contrary to theology since in all things it seeks those things which are its own and receives rather than gives something good. The first part is clear because the love of God which lives in man loves sinners, evil persons, fools, and weaklings in order to make them righteous, good, wise and strong. Rather than seeking its own good, the love of God flows forth and bestows good. Therefore sinners are attractive because they are loved; they are not loved because they are attractive. For this reason the love of man avoids sinners and evil persons. Thus Christ says: 'For I came not to call the righteous, but sinners' [*Matthew* IX: 13]. This is the love of the cross, born of the cross, which turns in the direction where it does not find good which it may enjoy, but where it may confer good upon the bad and needy person. 'It is more blessed to give than to receive' [*Acts* XX: 35], says the Apostle. Hence *Psalm* XLI [: 1] states, 'Blessed is he who considers the poor,' for the intellect cannot by nature comprehend an object which does not exist, that is the poor and needy person, but only a thing which does exist, that is the true and good. Therefore it judges according to appearances, is a respecter of persons, and judges according to that which can be seen, etc.

Amer. Edn. XXXI, 40 *et seq.*

F   THE ENCOUNTER WITH CAJETAN AT AUGSBURG, OCTOBER 1518

Luther's encounter with Cardinal Cajetan at Augsburg is one of the turning points in his career. At that moment he was in real danger of being repudiated by his friends, and abandoned by his prince. It was the first time he had had the chance to discuss his views with a theologian of the first rank, for Cajetan was the leading Thomist theologian of his age, and one of whose work modern historical theology speaks with increasing respect. The interview seems to have degenerated into a wrangle with both theologians shouting at one another, but it may be that Luther put his finger on a real weakness in the reference in the Bull *Unigenitus* to 'Christ acquired a treasure'. At any rate Cajetan saw to it that a further Papal pronouncement about Indulgences was forthcoming. Luther was also drawn into argument about the relation between faith and the promises of God in connection with the Sacrament of the Altar. Luther stood at this moment, or felt he did, in real personal danger and fled the city. The result was an angry account of the interview and of Luther's heretical character which Cajetan wrote to the Elector Frederick; this with Luther's reply, gives us a really extended account of the fateful confrontation. The vivid scene in John Osborne's *Luther* at this point seems to reach imaginative insight and is worth reading.

1   To George Spalatin, 10 October 1518

. . . Dear Spalatin, I arrived at Augsburg on 7 October. I arrived tired, for having contracted some grave stomach trouble, I almost fainted by the wayside, but I have recovered. This is the third day since I arrived, nor have I yet seen the very reverend lord legate, though on the very first day I sent Dr Wenzel Link and another to announce me. Meantime a safe-conduct is being secured for me by my friends from the imperial councillors. They are all very cordial to me for the sake of the illustrious Elector. But although the very reverend cardinal legate himself promises to treat me with all clemency, yet my friends will not allow me to rely on his word alone, so prudent and careful are they. For they know that he is inwardly enraged at me, no matter what he may outwardly pretend, and I myself clearly learned this elsewhere.

But today, at any rate, I shall approach him, and seek to see him and to have my first interview, though whether it will so turn out I do not know. . . . I know not whether the most reverend legate fears me or whether he is preparing some treachery.

Yesterday he sent to me the ambassador of Montferrat, to sound me on my position before the interview with himself. All think that the man came to me suborned and instructed by the legate, for he pleaded with me long, advancing arguments for sanity (as he called it), saying that I should simply agree with the legate, return to the Church, recant what I had said ill. He gave me the example of the Abbot Joachim of Flora who, by acting as he advised me to do, deserved to be considered no heretic, although he had uttered heresy. Then the suave gentleman dissuaded me from defending my opinions, asking if I wished to make it a tournament. In short, he is an Italian and an Italian he will remain. I said that if I could be shown that I had said anything contrary to the doctrine of the Holy Roman Church, I would soon be my own judge and recant. Our chief difficulty was that he cherished the opinions of Aquinas beyond what he can find authority for in the decrees of the Church. I will not yield to him on this point until the Church repeals her former decree on which I rely. 'Dear, dear,' said he, 'so you wish to have a tournament?' Then he went on to make some insane propositions, as, for example, he openly confessed that it was right to preach lies, if they were profitable and filled the chest. He denied that the power of the Pope should be treated in debate, but that it should be so exalted that the Pope might by his sole authority abrogate everything, including articles of faith, and especially that point we were now disputing on. He also made other propositions which I will tell you when I see you. But I dismissed this Sinon,[1] who too openly showed his Greek art, and he went away. Thus I hang between hope and fear, for this clumsy go-between did not give me the least confidence. . . .

The very reverend vicar John Staupitz writes that he will certainly come when he hears that I have arrived. . . .

AUGSBURG

Smith, Correspondence, I, 116 et seq.

2   To Andrew Karlstadt at Wittenberg, 14 October 1518

. . . For three days my affair has been in a hard case, so hard, indeed, that I had no hope of coming to you again and saw nothing ahead of

---

[1] The Greek who persuaded the Trojans to admit the wooden horse into their city, Virgil, *Aeneid*, II.79 *et seq.*

me more certain than excommunication. For all the while the legate would not allow me to debate publicly nor privately with him alone, meantime boasting that he will not be my judge, but will act as a father towards me in everything. Nonetheless, he will hear nothing from me except, 'I recant, I revoke, I confess that I erred', which I would not say.

Our chief difficulty was over two articles. (1) That I said Indulgence was not the treasury of the merits of our Lord and Saviour Christ. (2) That a man going to the sacrament must believe, etc.

Against these propositions the legate brought forward the decretal *Unigenitus*, relying on which he became extremely presumptuous as though I were wholly refuted and wished thereupon to force me to a recantation. . . .

AUGSBURG   Smith, *Correspondence*, I, 118 *et seq.*

3   The Pope's Political Difficulties: Pope Leo X to George Spalatin, 24 October 1518

At this crisis in the 'Luther affair' and at, as some think, the last moment when it might have been disposed of by the authorities, high politics intervened: the Pope found he badly needed the support of Frederick the Wise, as one of the seven Electors, in the struggle which now ensued on the death of the Emperor Maximilian and which was to result in the election of the young Charles V. At this moment, then, the Church authorities in Rome began to drag their feet, and one result was the mission of Charles von Miltitz to Germany.

Beloved Son, greeting and the Apostolic blessing! Considering the merits of the beloved and noble Frederic Elector of Saxony, and the favour which, following the custom of his famous ancestors, he has shown to us and the Apostolic See, and which he may show in greater measure hereafter, we have decided, with much affection and paternal love, to send him the most sacred golden rose, annually consecrated with mysterious rites on the fourth Sunday of Lent, and sent to some powerful Christian king or prince. We send it by our beloved son, Charles von Miltitz, our chamberlain and servant. We want you to know some things which concern the dignity and authority of us and of the aforesaid See.

For we know how much favour, and deservedly, you have with the said Elector, and how highly he considers your wholesome and prudent counsel. Wherefore we exhort you in the Lord, and paternally charge you on your duty and devotion to us and to the said See, that you consider how great an honour and gift we are sending the said Elector, and that you also consider how detestable is the overbearing boldness of that only son of Satan, Friar Martin Luther. Consider also that he savours of notorious heresy, and can blacken the name and fame of the great Elector and his ancestors. Take counsel then with our nuncio Miltitz, and try to persuade the said Elector to consult our dignity and that of our See, and his own honour. Let him crush the rashness of the said Luther, for his erroneous doctrines, now alas! widely sown among the credulous people, can only be extirpated by your aid and counsel. Your devotion to God, our Saviour, whose cause is now at stake, will be a special favour to us, whose chief care is to weed out the tares and cockle from the field of the Lord. You will always find us grateful and propitious to you, as you will learn more fully from Miltitz.

Given under the fisherman's ring, in the seventh year of our pontificate.

EVANGELISTA[1]

CIVITAVECCHIA

Smith, *Correspondence*, I, 127 *et seq.*

G THE LEIPZIG DISPUTATION, JUNE-JULY 1519

The Leipzig Disputation was, after the interview with Cajetan, Luther's most difficult and compromising public encounter before the Diet of Worms. It was complicated from the first by the entanglement between John Eck, Luther's most redoubtable opponent, and his senior colleague Andrew Karlstadt, who had provoked the initial challenge and who occupied the first week of the disputation with a long and tedious series of arguments about grace and free will. But if the whole thing came to life with Luther's intervention, Luther found himself on dangerous ground; for Eck fastened on the issue of Papal authority, and in particular succeeded in making Luther appear to defend articles put forward by the condemned heretic John Huss. The result was that to many Eck appeared to have gained a victory. Luther and his friends from Wittenberg, a serious and earnest-minded group, were disgusted at the apparent levity of the proceedings, and the evident sophistries of the other side. But what was more important, Luther himself had been driven into a corner, and forced

[1] One of the Papal secretaries.

to face implications of his teaching, in relation to Church authority, which he had perhaps not consciously hitherto admitted, and which in the next months were to press him into open defiance and disobedience.

1   Peter Mosellanus to Julius Pflug, 7 December 1519

. . . Both sides arrived promptly. Eck came with only a single personal servant, and with letters of introduction to our duke from the Fuggers. Luther and Karlstadt brought with them the greater part of their university, among their companions being Barnim, Duke of Pomerania, a modest youth loving letters and particularly gracious to me. Men of every estate gathered to see the debate, abbots, counts and knights, learned and unlearned, so that this large university had no hall big enough to accommodate such an audience. . . .

When the day set dawned, there was at six o'clock at St. Thomas's a magnificent mass for the success of the affair. Then in a splendid procession all hurried to the castle. To prevent a tumult armed guards were stationed at the doors. When all had come in and taken their assigned seats, I, poor man, in a fever, came in through the back door and ascended the platform, to speak, in the name of the duke, to the expectant audience. I confess that at first I was frightened by so great a concourse of prominent men, all expectant, and before so great a prince, whom I feared I would represent unworthily. Yet I spoke, if not with great applause, at least so that the duke and other grandees approved of it. When I came to the peroration, and all were anxiously expecting me to finish (for I spoke almost twice as long as usual), some musicians, prepared at my suggestion, were introduced through the same back door and started the hymn *Veni sancte Spiritus*, which they sang sweetly while the audience reverently kneeled. The time until noon having been consumed with these *preparations*, we went to lunch. A trumpet announced when to come back. All returned expectant.

Karlstadt and Eck, each asking the usual indulgence for himself, descended into the arena. They debated on free will, that is, what it has to do with the work of salvation. For Karlstadt sought to prove that whatever was meritorious in the words or deeds of a man was due wholly to God, and that man, of his own accord, could will nothing good, unless he received an influx of divine grace; in short, that God was the smith and our will the hammer with which he forged our salvation. Eck rebutted this opinion, which, if I understand aught in these matters, is by no means absurd. For almost three days he argued that merit was due partly to grace, partly to man's will. It finally came to this, that Eck conceded the whole good work was from God, but not wholly. This fine distinction Karlstadt not only confuted on the spot, but afterwards, in a long public letter, exposed as an invalid fiction.

Luther followed Karlstadt to sustain the thesis that it was only by recent decretals that the Roman Church was proved to be superior to other Churches, against which stood the authority of scripture and the Nicene Council. Eck left no stone unturned to overthrow this opinion; he summoned all the forces at his command, spending eight days on it and doing his best especially to make his opponent invidious by dragging in some Hussite articles. Luther at once understood the snare, and raged as though inspired by some spirit at being thus insidiously betrayed *on a side issue*. With great indignation he rejected some of the dogmas imputed to him, while embracing some of them as Christian, relying everywhere either on well weighed testimonies of scripture, or on the decrees of ancient councils. In short, his main effort was to remove far from himself the suspicion of favouring the Bohemian schism. Eck also bent his whole energy on impressing the audience with this opinion of Luther, no matter how much the latter rejected it. In like manner they debated on other things, the state of souls in purgatory, fear as the root of penitence, and Indulgences, consuming nearly twenty days in all.

When they had finished each side claimed the victory. Eck triumphs in the opinion of all who like *asses playing the harp* do not understand the subject at all, men who from boyhood have been brought up on Peter Hispanus, or who have some reason for wishing the Wittenbergers ill. The victory of Luther and Karlstadt is less acclaimed, because learned and judicious men are fewer and less confident in proclaiming their own opinions.

You have the story for which you asked, told briefly and in desultory manner, for I left out much not to the point. What? Don't you applaud? Perhaps I seem clumsy or *artificial* to you, or else you want more. I will give you portraits of the leaders in this war. Martin is of middle height with slender body worn out both by study and care, so that you can almost count his bones. He is in the vigour of manhood; his voice is sharp and clear. He is so wonderfully learned in the Bible that he has almost all the texts in memory. He has learned enough Greek and Hebrew to form a judgement of the translations. He has no lack of matter in speaking, for an immense stock of ideas and words are at his command. Perhaps you might miss in him judgement and method in using his stores. In daily life and manners he is cultivated and affable, having nothing of the stoic and nothing supercilious about him; rather he plays the man at all seasons. He is a joker in society, vivacious and sure, always with a happy face no matter how hard his enemies press him. You would hardly believe that he was the man to do such great things unless inspired by the gods. But what most men blame in him is that in answering he is more imprudent and cutting than is safe for *a reformer of the Church*, or than is decorous for a theologian. I know not whether this vice is not also common to the *pedants*.

Karlstadt is like Luther, but smaller. He is shorter, his face dark and burned, his voice thick and unpleasant, his memory is weaker and his anger more prompt.

Eck has a tall stature, a solid, square body, a full, German voice, strong lungs as of a tragedian or cryer, but emitting a rough rather than clear sound. So far is he from having that native sweetness of the Latin tongue, praised by Fabius and Cicero! His mouth and eyes, or rather his whole face, would make you think him a butcher or Carian soldier rather than a theologian. He has a fine memory; were his understanding only equal to it he would possess all nature's gifts. The man cannot grasp a thing quickly nor judge it acutely, so that his other talents are vain. This is the reason why in debate he brings together all his arguments and texts of scripture and quotations from authors without any selection, not considering that many of them are inept and impertinent to the subject, and that some are *apocryphal* or mere sophistry. He only tries to discharge a copious mass of matter, thus deceiving his audience, most of whom are stupid, and from whom he thus wins the opinion that he is victor. Add to this incredible audacity covered by admirable craft. If he thinks he is falling into the snares of his adversary, he turns the debate into another channel, sometimes embracing his opponent's opinion, clothed in other words, as his own, and, with equal guile, imputing his own absurdities to his antagonist. . . .

MEISSEN

Smith, *Correspondence*, I, 257 *et seq.*

2   The Condemnation of Luther: from the Bull 'Exsurge Domine' of Pope Leo X, 15 June 1520

Arise O Lord and judge thy cause. . . . Arise O Peter, and in the name of the pastoral charge committed to thee from on high, put forth they strength in the cause of the holy Roman Church, the mother of all churches, the mistress of the faith. . . . Arise thou also, O Paul, we beg thee, who hast enlightened her with thy teaching. . . . In a word, let every saint arise and the whole remaining universal Church. . . . Let intercession be made to almighty God, that his sheep may be purged of their errors and every heresy be expelled from the confines of the faithful, and that God may deign to preserve the peace and unity of his holy Church. . . .

For some time we have been hearing of, or rather, alas!, seeing and reading with our own eyes, many different errors which, although in part condemned aforetimes by councils and decisions of our predecessors . . . , have been stirred up afresh, and latterly . . . sown abroad in the renowned nation of Germany. . . . We cannot, in view of our pastoral office, laid on us by divine grace, any longer tolerate the poisonous virus of these errors. . . . [*The list follows*]

1   It is an heretical but commonly held opinion that the sacraments of the New Law gives justifying grace to those who place no obstacle in its way.

2   To deny that sin remains in a child after baptism is to trample on (the teaching of) Paul and Christ alike.

3   The capacity of sinning [*fomes peccati*, literally the 'tinder of sin'], even where no actual sin is present, hinders the soul, as it leaves the body, from entering heaven.

4   The imperfect love of a dying man cannot but produce a great fear, which of itself is enough to constitute the penalty of purgatory; and this hinders entrance into the kingdom.

5   The threefold division of penitence into contrition, confession and satisfaction, is based neither on holy scripture nor the writings of the ancient and holy Christian doctors.

6   The contrition which results from discussion, comparison and detestation of one's sins, and with which one reviews one's past years in bitterness of soul, weighing the gravity, multitude, hideousness of the sins – the forfeiting of eternal blessedness, the procuring of eternal damnation – such contrition makes of one a hypocrite and a worse sinner than before.

7   Truest of all, and worth more than all that has been taught to date about contritions, is the proverb: 'Penitence at its highest is – not to do it again; penitence at its best is – a new life.'

8   You must not in the least presume to confess venial sins – nor all
your mortal sins, either, for you cannot possibly have cognizance of
them all. This is why in the primitive church the only mortal sins
confessed were those committed for all to see.

9   Our purpose to make pure confession of everything really only
means that we want there to be nothing left for the divine mercy to
pardon.

10   No sins are remitted unless, when the priest pronounces absolution, a man *believes* that they are remitted; . . .

11   You are on no account to believe that absolution is due to your
contrition, but rather to the Word of Christ ('Whatsoever ye shall
loose . . .' [*Matthew* xvi: 19]). . . .

12   If, to take an impossible case, a confessor were not contrite, or the
priest were not serious but joking in his absolution, nevertheless if
he believes he is absolved, then absolved he is in very truth.

13   In the sacrament of penance or the remission of guilt, the Pope or
the bishop does no more than the lowliest priest; indeed, when there
is no priest, any Christian – even a woman or a child – could do
the same.

14   No one is bound to reply to the priest that he is contrite, nor the
priest to ask it.

15   They are greatly in error who approach the Eucharist relying on
their confession of sin, on their consciousness of no mortal sin, or
their due performance of prayers and preparations: all such eat and
drink to their own judgement. But if they believe and trust that
there they will find grace, this faith alone (*sola fides*) makes them
pure and worthy.

16   It is apparently agreed that the Church should decree by a general
Council that the laity should be communicated in both kinds:[1] the
Bohemians, who follow this practice, are not heretics – merely
schismatics.

17   The treasures of the Church, whence the Pope grants Indulgences,
are *not* the merits of Christ and the saints. . . .

19   Indulgences, even when sincerely sought, have no power for the
remission of the punishment which divine justice awards actual
sins. . . .

[1] In other words, the wine as well as the bread.

21 Indulgences are only necessary for public crimes, and are properly granted only to hardened and unfeeling offenders. . . .

23 Excommunication is a mere external penalty; it does not deprive a man of the common spiritual prayers of the Church. . . .

25 The Roman Pontiff, the successor of Peter, is *not* the Vicar of Christ over all the churches in the whole world, appointed as such by Christ himself in blessed Peter.

26 The word of Christ to Peter: 'Whatsoever thou loosest on earth' etc. [*Matthew* XVI] applies only to Peter's own binding (and loosing).

27 It is certain that it is not in the power of Church or Pope to fix articles of faith, or even laws of conduct or of good works.

28 If the Pope, supported by a large part of the Church, expresses this or that opinion – and a correct one at that: even so, it is neither sin nor heresy to disagree, especially if the matter is not one necessary to salvation, until a universal Council has approved the one view and condemned the other.

29 It is open to us to weaken the authority of Councils, freely to contradict their findings, to sit in judgement on their decrees, and to confess with boldness whatever appears to us to be true, whether any Council has approved or condemned it.

30 Certain articles of John Huss, condemned by the Council of Constance, are most Christian, true, and evangelical; the universal Church could not possibly condemn them.

31 In every good work a righteous man sins.

32 A good work perfectly executed is – a venial sin.

33 To burn heretics is contrary to the will of the Spirit.

34 To fight the Turks is to resist God, who is visiting our sins upon us through them.

35 No one can be sure that he is not always sinning mortally, because of the hidden and secret vice of pride.

36 Free will after sin is a mere name; while it does what in it lies it sins mortally.

37 Purgatory cannot be proved by the canonical sacred scriptures.

38 Souls in purgatory have no assurance of their salvation – at least, not all of them. . . .

39   Souls in purgatory sin without intermission as long as they look
for rest and recoil from punishment.

40   Souls released from purgatory receive less blessing from the intercessions of the living than if they had given satisfaction of themselves.

Latin in Kidd, Doc. 38*

3   To Spalatin (between 12 and 18 February 1520)

Greeting. Good heavens! Spalatin, how excited you are! More than I
or anyone else. I wrote to you before not to assume that this affair was
begun or is carried on by your judgement or mine or that of any man.
If it is of God, it will be completed contrary to, outside of, above and
below, your or my understanding.

But let me tell you again that I would not have the least part of this
cause decided by your fate or by mine, and that my only fear has always
been that I should be left to myself and thus write what would please
human wisdom. You must beware of being too wise and I of being too
foolish. Too much folly, I confess, displeases men, but too much wisdom still more displeases God, who has chosen the foolish things of the
world to confound the wise.

You do not see that my long suffering in not answering five or six
wagonloads of Emser's and Eck's curses was the sole cause why those
bloated makers of placards dared to revile me with their ridiculous folly.

Secondly, I know that I do not care that at Leipzig my sermon was
forbidden and suppressed in a public edict, for I despise their suspicion,
reproaches, injuries and malice. Forsooth must we allow these bold
men to add to their other furious acts the publication of libels, stuffed
not only with lies, but with blasphemy against the Gospel truth? Do
you forbid us even to bark against these wolves?

The Lord is my witness, how much I have restrained myself for the
sake of the bishop's name, not to treat this cursed and impotent edict
irreverently. I shall say elsewhere what their brains ought to hear, when
they acknowledge that they have published the edict and begin to
defend themselves. I consider them unpeaceable and in a future tract
shall not abstain from treating them as violators of law, Gospel, and
common sense, so that they may know how much I have hitherto
spared their ignorance and malice.

I see that you have not read the edict with sufficient care. If they were not more ignorant than any asses, they would know that nothing was ever written against me, or rather against God's word, more venomous, pestilent, malignant and mendacious. On this account should we exult, or change our manner of writing, or suffer more? You know how I despise that inconvenience.

If you think properly of the Gospel, please do not imagine that its cause can be advanced without tumult, offence and sedition. You will not make a pen from a sword, nor peace of war. The Word of God is a sword, it is war and ruin and offence and perdition and poison, and, as Amos says, it met the sons of Ephraim as a bear in the way and as a lioness in the wood. I wrote much more vehemently against Emser, Eck and Tetzel, and you never complained. What if even the official or the bishop himself does not acknowledge publishing the edict?

They write in greater danger than I do, for they have so forgotten all Gospel, laws, reason and common sense, that they care for nothing but to condemn me unheard, unwarned and untaught. . . .

If I am immoderate, at least I am simple and open, in which I think I am better than they who invent stories full of guile. Farewell and fear not.

WITTENBERG   BROTHER MARTIN LUTHER
                                    Smith, *Correspondence*, I, 286 *et seq.*

H   THE MANIFESTOS OF 1520

Luther's famous three treatises of 1520 were the manifestos of the German Reformation. The first, the appeal to the Christian nobility of the German nation is an unwieldy compilation, for it includes a great many familiar grumbles and grievances of the Germans against Rome. But it was addressed to all classes in Germany, from the young Emperor Charles to the princes, knights and common people and it found an immediate response in all classes. This was the transitory moment when it seemed that Luther's revolt might indeed unite Germany, according to some historians. Theologically this document announces Luther's doctrine of the 'priesthood of all believers', on the basis of which he appeals to the temporal authorities to intervene and take in hand the reform which the spiritual authorities have failed to do. The second treatise, unlike the first, was in Latin, and addressed to the clergy and the humanists; it marks the point where reform turns to revolution in his hands in his attack on the sources of clerical power and on the seven sacraments. The third tract *Of the Liberty of a Christian Man* – dedicated to the Pope at this eleventh hour, is a classic, an exposition of how the life of faith is one of Christian liberty, issuing creatively and spontaneously in loving service of our neighbours. It is best read together with Luther's sermon *On Good Works* of a few months before.

1   'To the Christian Nobility of the German Nation Respecting the Reformation of the Christian Estate'

The time for silence is gone, and the time to speak has come, as we read in *Ecclesiastes* [III: 7]. I have, in conformity with our resolve, put together some few points concerning the reformation of the Christian estate, with the intent of placing the same before the Christian nobility of the German nation, in case it may please God to help his Church by means of the laity, inasmuch as the clergy, whom this task rather befitted, have become quite careless. . . .

The distress and misery that oppress all the Christian estates, more especially in Germany, have led not only myself, but every one else, to cry aloud and to ask for help, and have now forced me too to cry out and to ask if God would give his Spirit to any one to reach a hand to his wretched people. . . .

We must renounce all confidence in our natural strength, and take the matter in hand with humble trust in God; we must seek God's help with earnest prayer, and have nothing before our eyes but the misery and wretchedness of Christendom, irrespective of what punishment the wicked may deserve. If we do not act thus, we may begin the game with great pomp; but when we are well in it, the spirits of evil will make such confusion that the whole world will be immersed in blood, and yet nothing be done. . . .

The Romanists have, with great adroitness, drawn three walls round themselves, with which they have hitherto protected themselves, so that no one could reform them, whereby all Christendom has fallen terribly.

Firstly, if pressed by the temporal power, they have affirmed and maintained that the temporal power has no jurisdiction over them, but, on the contrary, that the spiritual power is above the temporal.

Secondly, if it were proposed to admonish them with the scriptures, they objected that no one may interpret the scriptures but the Pope.

Thirdly, if they are threatened with a council, they pretend that no one may call a council but the Pope. . . .

(a) *The First Wall*

Let us, in the first place, attack the first wall.

It has been devised that the Pope, bishops, priests and monks are called the spiritual estate; princes, lords, artificers and peasants are the temporal estate. This is an artful lie and hypocritical device, but let no one be made afraid by it, and that for this reason: that all Christians are truly of the spiritual estate, and there is no difference among them, save of office alone. As St. Paul says [*I Corinthians* xii], we are all one body, though each member does its own work, to serve the others. This is because we have one baptism, one Gospel, one faith, and are all Christians alike; for baptism, Gospel and faith, these alone make spiritual and Christian people. . . .

Thus we are all consecrated as priests by baptism, as St. Peter says: 'Ye are a royal priesthood, a holy nation' [*I Peter* ii:9]; and in the *Book of Revelation*: 'and hast made us unto our God (by thy blood) kings and priests' [*Revelation* v:10]. For, if we had not a higher consecration in us than Pope or bishop can give, no priest could ever be made by the consecration of Pope or bishop, nor could he say the mass, or preach, or absolve. Therefore the bishop's consecration is just as if the name of the whole congregation he took one person out of the community, each member of which has equal power, and commanded him to exercise this power for the rest; in the same way as if ten brothers, co-heirs as king's sons, were to choose one from among them to rule over their inheritance, they would all of them still remain kings and have equal power, although one is ordered to govern.

And to put the matter even more plainly, if a little company of pious Christian laymen were taken prisoners and carried away to a desert, and had not among them a priest consecrated by a bishop, and were there to agree to elect one of them, born in wedlock or not, and were to order him to baptize, to celebrate the mass, to absolve, and to preach, this man would as truly be a priest, as if all the bishops and all the Popes had consecrated him. That is why in cases of necessity every man can baptize and absolve, which would not be possible if we were not all priests. This great grace and virtue of baptism and of the Christian estate they have quite destroyed and made us forget by their ecclesiastical law. . . .

Since, then, the temporal power is baptized as we are, and has the same faith and Gospel, we must allow it to be priest and bishop, and account its office an office that is proper and useful to the Christian community. For whatever issues from baptism may boast that it has been consecrated priest, bishop and Pope, although it does not beseem every one to exercise these offices. For, since we are all priests alike, no man may put himself forward or take upon himself, without our consent and election, to do that which we have all alike power to do. For, if a thing is common to all, no man may take it to himself without the wish and command of the community. And if it should happen that a man were appointed to one of these offices and deposed for abuses, he would be just what he was before. Therefore a priest should be nothing in Christendom but a functionary; as long as he holds his office, he has precedence of others; if he is deprived of it, he is a peasant or a citizen like the rest. Therefore a priest is verily no longer a priest after deposition. But now they have invented *characteres indelebiles* and pretend that a priest after deprivation still differs from a simple layman. They even imagine that a priest can never become a layman. All this is nothing but mere talk and ordinance of human invention.

It follows, then, that between laymen and priests, princes and bishops, or, as they call it, between spiritual and temporal persons, the only real difference is one of office and function, and not of estate; for they are all of the same spiritual estate, true priests, bishops and Popes, though their functions are not the same – just as among priests and monks every man has not the same functions. And this, as I said above, St. Paul says [*Romans* xii; *I Corinthians* xii], and St. Peter [*I Peter* ii]: 'We, being many, are one body in Christ, and severally members, one of another.' Christ's body is not double or twofold, one temporal, the other spiritual. He is one Head, and he has one body. . . .

In the same way the temporal authorities hold the sword and the rod in their hands to punish the wicked and to protect the good. A cobbler, a smith, a peasant, every man has the office and function of his calling, and yet all alike are consecrated priests and bishops, and every man should by his office or function be useful and beneficial to the rest, so that various kinds of work may all be united for the furtherance of body and soul, just as the members of the body all serve one another. . . .

(b) The Second Wall

. . . Therefore it is a wickedly devised fable – and they cannot quote a single letter to confirm it – that it is for the Pope alone to interpret the scriptures or to confirm the interpretation of them. They have assumed the authority of their own selves. And though they say that this authority was given to St. Peter when the keys were given to him, it is plain enough that the keys were not given to St. Peter alone, but to the whole community. . . .

(c) The Third Wall

... They can show nothing in the scriptures giving the Pope sole power to call and confirm councils; they have nothing but their own laws; but these hold good only so long as they are not injurious to Christianity and the laws of God. ...

Therefore when need requires, and the Pope is a cause of offence to Christendom, in these cases whoever can best do so, as a faithful member of the whole body, must do what he can to procure a true free council. This no one can do so well as the temporal authorities, especially since they are fellow-Christians, fellow-priests, sharing one spirit and one power in all things, and since they should exercise the office that they have received from God without hindrance, whenever it is necessary and useful that it should be exercised. Would it not be most unnatural, if a fire were to break out in a city, and every one were to keep still and let it burn on and on, whatever might be burnt, simply because they had not the mayor's authority, or because the fire perchance broke out at the mayor's house? Is not every citizen bound in this case to rouse and call in the rest? How much more should this be done in the spiritual city of Christ, if a fire of offence breaks out, either at the Pope's government or wherever it may! The like happens if an enemy attacks a town. The first to rouse up the rest earns glory and thanks. Why then should not he earn glory that descries the coming of our enemies from hell and rouses and summons all Christians? ...

Therefore we learn from the Apostle clearly, that every town should elect a pious learned citizen from the congregation and charge him with the office of minister; the congregation should support him, and he should be left at liberty to marry or not. He should have as assistants several priests and deacons, married or not, as they please, who should help him to govern the people and the congregation with sermons and the ministration of the sacraments, as is still the case in the Greek Church. ...

What are the universities, as at present ordered, but, as the book of Maccabees says, schools of Greek fashion and heathenish manners [*II Maccabees* IV: 12, 13], full of dissolute living, where very little is taught of the holy scriptures and of the Christian faith, and the blind heathen teacher, Aristotle, rules even further than Christ? Now, my advice would be that the books of Aristotle, the *Physics*, the *Metaphysics*, *Of the Soul*, *Ethics*, which have hitherto been considered the best, be altogether abolished, with all others that profess to treat of nature, though nothing can be learned from them, either of natural or of spiritual things. Besides, no one has been able to understand his meaning, and much time has been wasted and many noble souls vexed with much useless labour, study and expense. I venture to say that any potter has more knowledge of natural things than is to be found in these books. My heart is grieved to see how many of the best Christians this accursed, proud, knavish heathen has fooled and led astray with his false words. God sent him as a plague for our sins. . . .

Then there is the *Ethics*, which is accounted one of the best, though no book is more contrary directly to God's will and the Christian virtues. Oh that such books could be kept out of the reach of all Christians! Let no one object that I say too much, or speak without knowledge. My friend, I know of what I speak. I know Aristotle as well as you or men like you. I have read him with more understanding than St. Thomas or Scotus, which I may say without arrogance, and can prove if need be. It matters not that so many great minds have exercised themselves in these matters for many hundred years. Such objections do not affect me as they might have done once, since it is plain as day that many more errors have existed for many hundred years in the world and the universities.

I would, however, gladly consent that Aristotle's books of *Logic*, *Rhetoric*, and *Poetry* should be retained, or they might be usefully studied in a condensed form, to practise young people in speaking and preaching; but the notes and comments should be abolished, and, just as Cicero's *Rhetoric* is read without note or comment, Aristotle's *Logic* should be read without such long commentaries. But now neither speaking nor preaching is taught out of them, and they are used only for disputation and toilsomeness. Besides this, there are languages – Latin, Greek, and Hebrew – the mathematics, history; which I recommend to men of higher understanding: and other matters, which will come of themselves, if they seriously strive after reform. And truly it is an important matter, for it concerns the teaching and training of Christian youths and of our noble people, in whom Christianity still abides. Therefore I think that Pope and emperor could have no better task than the reformation of the universities, just as there is nothing more devilishly mischievous than an unreformed university.

I should have thought that young theologians might begin by studying the *Sentences*, and that doctors should study the Bible. Now they invert this: the Bible is the first thing they study; this ceases with the Bachelor's degree; the *Sentences* are the last, and these they keep for ever with the Doctor's degree, and this, too, under such sacred obligation that one that is not a priest may read the Bible, but a priest must read the *Sentences*; so that, as far as I can see a married man might be a doctor in the Bible, but not in the *Sentences*. How should we prosper so long as we act so perversely, and degrade the Bible, the holy word of God? . . .

Above all, in schools of all kinds the chief and most common lesson should be the scriptures, and for young boys the Gospel; and would to God each town had also a girls' school, in which girls might be taught the Gospel for an hour daily, either in German or Latin! . . .

Should not every Christian be expected by his ninth or tenth year to know all the holy Gospels, containing as they do his very name and life? A spinner or a seamstress teaches her daughter her trade while she is young, but now even the most learned prelates and bishops do not know the Gospel. . . .

I have frequently offered to submit my writings for inquiry and examination, but in vain, though I know, if I am in the right, I must be condemned upon earth and justified by Christ alone in heaven. For all the scriptures teach us that the affairs of Christians and Christendom must be judged by God alone; they have never yet been justified by men in this world, but the opposition has always been too strong. My greatest care and fear is lest my cause be not condemned by men, by which I should know for certain that it does not please God. Therefore let them go freely to work, Pope, bishop, priest, monk, or doctor; they are the true people to persecute the truth, as they have always done. May God grant us all a Christian understanding, and especially to the Christian nobility of the German nation true spiritual courage, to do what is best for our unhappy Church. Amen! . . .

On the Sacrament of Extreme Unction
To this rite of anointing the sick our theologians have made two additions well worthy of themselves. One is that they call it a Sacrament, the other that they make it extreme, so that it cannot be administered except to those who are in extreme peril of life. . . .

Wace and Buchheim, 17-92, 237

2 'On the Babylonish Captivity of the Church'

I must deny that there are seven Sacraments, and must lay it down, for the time being, that there are only three, baptism, penance and the bread, and that by the court of Rome all these have been brought into miserable bondage, and the Church despoiled of all her liberty. And yet, if I were to speak according to the usage of scripture, I should hold that there was only one Sacrament, and three Sacramental signs. I shall speak on this point more at length at the proper time; but now I speak of the sacrament of the bread, the first of all. . . .

Formerly, when I was imbibing the scholastic theology, my lord the Cardinal of Cambray gave me occasion for reflection by arguing most acutely, in the fourth book of the *Sentences*, that it would be much more probable, and that fewer superfluous miracles would have to be introduced, if real bread and real wine, and not only their accidents, were understood to be upon the altar, unless the Church had determined the contrary. Afterwards, when I saw what the Church was which had thus determined – namely, the Thomistic, that is, the Aristotelian Church – I became bolder; and whereas I had been before in great straits of doubt, I now at length established my conscience in the former opinion, namely, that there is real bread and real wine, in which is the real flesh and real blood of Christ, in no other manner and in no less degree than the other party assert them to be under the accidents. . . .

I quite consent, then, that whoever chooses to hold either opinion should do so. My only object now is to remove scruples of conscience, so that no man may fear being guilty of heresy if he believes that real bread and real wine are present on the altar. . . .

But why should not Christ be able to include His body within the substance of bread, as well as within the accidents? Fire and iron, two different substances, are so mingled in red-hot iron that every part of it is both fire and iron. Why may not the glorious body of Christ much more be in every part of the substance of the bread? . . .

The third bondage of this same Sacrament is that abuse of it – and by far the most impious – by which it has come about that at this day there is no belief in the Church more generally received or more firmly held than that the mass is a good work and a sacrifice. This abuse has brought in an infinite flood of other abuses, until faith in the Sacrament has been utterly lost, and they have made this divine Sacrament a mere subject of traffic, huckstering, and money-getting contracts. . . .

Concerning the Sacrament of Baptism

. . . This doctrine ought to have been studiously inculcated upon the people by preaching; this promise ought to have been perpetually reiterated; men ought to have been constantly reminded of their baptism; faith ought to have been called forth and nourished. When this divine promise has been once conferred upon us, its truth continues even to the hour of our death; and thus our faith in it ought never to be relaxed, but ought to be nourished and strengthened, even till we die, by perpetual recollection of the promise made to us in baptism. . . .

From what has been said we may clearly distinguish between man, the minister, and God, the Author, of baptism. Man baptizes, and does not baptize: he baptizes, because he performs the work of dipping the baptized person; he does not baptize, because in this work he does not act upon his own authority, but in the place of God. Hence we ought to receive baptism from the hand of man just as if Christ himself, nay, God himself, were baptizing us with his own hands. For it is not a man's baptism, but that of Christ and God, though we receive it by the hand of a man. . . .

Baptism then signifies two things: death and resurrection; that is, full and complete justification. When the minister dips the child into the water, this signifies death; when he draws him out again, this signifies life.

Concerning the Sacrament of Penance

. . . When Christ says, 'Whatsoever ye shall bind', etc., he means to call forth the faith of the penitent man, so that, on the strength of this work of promise, he may be sure that, if he believes and is absolved, he will be truly absolved in heaven. Evidently nothing is said here of power, but it is the ministry of absolution which is spoken of. It is strange enough that these blind and arrogant men have not arrogated to themselves some tyrannical power from the terms of the baptismal promise. If not, why have they presumed to do so from the promise connected with penitence? In both cases there is an equal ministry, a like promise, and the same character in the Sacrament; and it cannot be denied that, if we do not owe baptism to Peter alone, it is a piece of impious tyranny to claim the power of the keys for the Pope alone. . . .

Of Confirmation

It is surprising how it should have entered anyone's mind to make a Sacrament of confirmation out of that laying on of hands which Christ applied to little children, and by which the Apostles bestowed the Holy Spirit, ordained presbyters, and healed the sick, as the Apostle writes to Timothy, 'Lay hands suddenly on no man'. . . .

I do not say this because I condemn the seven Sacraments but because I deny that they can be proved from the scriptures. . . .

Of Matrimony

It is not only without any warrant of scripture that matrimony is considered a Sacrament, but it has been turned into a mere mockery by the very same traditions which vaunt it as a Sacrament. . . .

Of Orders

Of this Sacrament the Church of Christ knows nothing: it was invented by the Church of the Pope. It not only has no promise of grace, anywhere declared, but not a word is said about it in the whole of the New Testament. Now it is ridiculous to set up as a Sacrament of God that which can nowhere be proved to have been instituted by God. Not that I consider that a rite practised for so many ages is to be condemned; but I would not have human invention established in sacred things, nor should it be allowed to bring in anything as divinely ordained which has not been divinely ordained, lest we should be objects of ridicule to our adversaries. . . .

Let every man then who has learnt that he is a Christian recognize what he is, and be certain that we are all equally priests, that is that we have the same power in the word, and in any sacrament whatever, although it is not lawful for any one to use this power, except with the consent of the community. . . .

Wace and Buchheim, 147-235

3   'Concerning Christian Liberty'

. . . I first lay down these two propositions, concerning spiritual liberty and servitude: a Christian man is the most free lord of all, and subject to none; a Christian man is the most dutiful servant of all, and subject to everyone. . . .

Man is composed of a twofold nature, a spiritual and a bodily. As regards the spiritual nature, which they name the soul, he is called the spiritual, inward, new man; as regards the bodily nature, which they name the flesh, he is called the fleshly, outward, old man. The Apostle speaks of this: 'Though our outward man perish, yet the inward man is renewed day by day [*II Corinthians* IV: 16]. The result of this diversity is that in the scriptures opposing statements are made concerning the same man, the fact being that in the same man these two men are opposed to one another; the flesh lusting against the spirit, and the spirit against the flesh [*Galatians* V: 17]. . . .

And so it will profit nothing that the body should be adorned with sacred vestments, or dwell in holy places, or be occupied in sacred offices, or pray, fast and abstain from certain meats, or do whatever works can be done through the body and in the body. Something widely different will be necessary for the justification and liberty of the soul, since the things I have spoken of can be done by any impious person, and only hypocrites are produced by devotion to those things. On the other hand, it will not at all injure the soul that the body should be clothed in profane raiment, should dwell in profane places, should eat and drink in the ordinary fashion, should not pray aloud, and should leave undone all the things above mentioned, which may be done by hypocrites.

And, to cast everything aside, even speculations, meditations, and whatever things can be performed by the exertions of the soul itself, are of no profit. One thing, and one alone, is necessary for life, justification and Christian liberty; and that is the most holy word of God, the Gospel of Christ. . . .

Let us therefore hold it for certain and firmly established that the soul can do without everything except the word of God, without which none at all of its wants are provided for. But, having the word, it is rich and wants for nothing. . . .

Hence it is clear that as the soul needs the word alone for life and justification, so it is justified by faith alone, and not by any works. . . .

Meanwhile it is to be noted that the whole scripture of God is divided into two parts: precepts and promises. The precepts certainly teach us what is good, but what they teach is not forthwith done. For they show us what we ought to do, but do not give us the power to do it. They were ordained, however, for the purpose of showing man to himself, that through them he may learn his own impotence for good and may despair of his own strength. For this reason they are called the Old Testament, and are so. . . .

Hence the promises of God belong to the New Testament; nay, are the New Testament.

Now, since these promises of God are words of holiness, truth, righteousness, liberty, and peace, and are full of universal goodness, the soul, which cleaves to them with a firm faith, is so united to them, nay, thoroughly absorbed by them, that it not only partakes in, but is penetrated and saturated by, all their virtues. . . .

From all this it is easy to understand why faith has such great power, and why no good works, nor even all good works put together, can compare with it, since no work can cleave to the word of God or be in the soul. Faith alone and the word reign in it; and such as is the word, such is the soul made by it, just as iron exposed to fire glows like fire, on account of its union with the fire. . . .

This is that Christian liberty, our faith, the effect of which is, not that we should be careless or lead a bad life, but that no one should need the law or works for justification and salvation.

Let us consider this as the first virtue of faith; and let us look also to the second. This also is an office of faith: that it honours with the utmost veneration and the highest reputation him in whom it believes, inasmuch as it holds him to be truthful and worthy of belief. . . .

The third incomparable grace of faith is this: that it unites the soul to Christ, as the wife to the husband, by which mystery, as the Apostle teaches, Christ and the soul are made one flesh. . . .

If we compare these possessions, we shall see how inestimable is the gain. Christ is full of grace, life, and salvation; the soul is full of sin, death, and condemnation. Let faith step in, and then sin, death and hell will belong to Christ, and grace, life and salvation to the soul. For, if he is a husband, he must needs take to himself that which is his wife's, and, at the same time, impart to his wife that which is his. . . .

Nor are we only kings and the freest of all men, but also priests for ever, a dignity far higher than kingship, because by that priesthood we are worthy to appear before God, to pray for others, and to teach one another mutually the things which are of God. For these are the duties of priests, and they cannot possibly be permitted to any unbeliever. Christ has obtained for us this favour, if we believe in him. . . .

Here you will ask, 'If all who are in the Church are priests, by what character are those whom we now call priests to be distinguished from the laity?' I reply, that by the use of these words, 'priest', 'clergy', 'spiritual person', 'ecclesiastic', an injustice has been done, since they have been transferred from the remaining body of Christians to those few who are now, by a hurtful custom, called ecclesiastics. For holy scripture makes no distinction between them, except that those who are now boastfully called Popes, bishops, and lords, it calls ministers, servants, and stewards, who are to serve the rest in the ministry of the word, for teaching the faith of Christ and the liberty of believers.

And now let us turn to the other part: to the outward man. . . . Here then works begin; here he must not take his ease; here he must give heed to exercise his body by fastings, watchings, labour and other regular discipline, so that it may be subdued to the spirit, and obey and conform itself to the inner man and faith, and not rebel against them nor hinder them, as is its nature to do if it is not kept under. For the inner man, being conformed to God and created after the image of God through faith, rejoices and delights itself in Christ, in whom such blessings have been conferred on it, and hence has only this task before it: to serve God with joy and for nought in free love. . . .

As Christ says, 'A good tree cannot bring forth evil fruit, neither can a corrupt tree bring forth good fruit' [*Matthew* VII:18]. Now it is clear that the fruit does not bear the tree, nor does the tree grow on the fruit; but, on the contrary, the trees bear the fruit, and the fruit grows on the trees.

As then trees must exist before their fruit, and as the fruit does not make the tree either good or bad, but, on the contrary, a tree of either kind produces fruit of the same kind, so must first the person of the man be good or bad before he can do either a good or a bad work; and his works do not make him bad or good, but he himself makes his works either bad or good. . . .

We do not then reject good works; nay, we embrace them and teach them in the highest degree. It is not on their own account that we condemn them, but on account of this impious addition to them and the perverse notion of seeking justification by them. . . .

Lastly, we will speak also of those works which he performs towards his neighbour. For man does not live for himself alone in this mortal body, in order to work on its account, but also for all men on earth; nay, he lives only for others, and not for himself. For it is to this end that he brings his own body into subjection, that he may be able to serve others more sincerely and more freely. . . .

Thus it is impossible that he should take his ease in this life, and not work for the good of his neighbours, since he must needs speak, act, and converse among men, just as Christ was made in the likeness of men and found in fashion as a man, and had his conversation among men. . . .

It is the part of a Christian to take care of his own body for the very purpose that, by its soundness and well-being, he may be enabled to labour, and to acquire and preserve property, for the aid of those who are in want, that thus the stronger member may serve the weaker member, and we may be children of God, thoughtful and busy one for another, bearing one another's burdens, and so fulfilling the law of Christ. . . .

In this we see clearly that the Apostle lays down this rule for a Christian life that all our works should be directed to the advantage of others, since every Christian has such abundance through his faith that all his other works and his whole life remain over and above wherewith to serve and benefit his neighbour of spontaneous goodwill. . . .

C

Though he is thus free from all works, yet he ought to empty himself of this liberty, take on him the form of a servant, be made in the likeness of men, be found in fashion as a man, serve, help, and in every way act towards his neighbour as he sees that God through Christ has acted and is acting towards him. All this he should do freely, and with regard to nothing but the good pleasure of God, and he should reason thus:

'Lo! my God, without merit on my part, of his pure and free mercy, has given to me, an unworthy, condemned and contemptible creature, all the riches of justification and salvation in Christ, so that I no longer am in want of anything, except of faith to believe that this is so. For such a Father, then, who has overwhelmed me with these inestimable riches of his, why should I not freely, cheerfully, and with my whole heart and from voluntary zeal, do all that I know will be pleasing to him and acceptable in his sight? I will therefore give myself, as a sort of Christ, to my neighbour, as Christ has given himself to me; and will do nothing in this life except what I see will be needful, advantageous and wholesome for my neighbour, since by faith I should abound in all good things in Christ.'

Thus from faith flow forth love and joy in the Lord, and from love a cheerful, willing, free spirit, disposed to serve our neighbour voluntarily, without taking any account of gratitude or ingratitude, praise or blame, gain or loss. Its object is not to lay men under obligations, nor does it distinguish between friends and enemies, or look to gratitude or ingratitude, but most freely and willingly spends itself and its goods, whether it loses them through ingratitude, or gains goodwill. For thus did its Father, distributing all things to all men abundantly and freely, making his sun to rise upon the just and the unjust. Thus, too, the child does and endures nothing except from the free joy with which it delights through Christ in God, the giver of such great gifts. . . .

Wace and Buchheim, 104-28

4   Aleander to Cardinal de Medici, 8 February 1521

. . . But now the whole of Germany is in full revolt; nine-tenths raise the war-cry, 'Luther!', while the watchword of the other tenth who are indifferent to Luther, is: 'Death to the Roman Curia!' . . . The bull accrediting me, and giving me power to name representatives, should be sent; also the breves to the persons I already mentioned, and numerous letters of introduction to princes and bishops, together with fifty copies of the bull of condemnation to give to bishops and prelates, and money for my expenses and for secretaries and agents. Even if they are all much exasperated against us, yet a handful of gold will make them dance to our pipe, though even thus it is hard to win them, and impossible in any other way. . . .

I am very sorry that the word of Erasmus, who has written worse things against our faith than has Luther, should be more trusted than mine, though I let myself be torn in pieces for this faith. But this Erasmus knows his own advantage, like a faithless wife who gives her husband a sharp scolding before she makes him a cuckold. I have long known that Erasmus is the source of all this evil which he has scattered around Flanders and the Rhine land, but I have refrained from saying so and have instead rather always praised him and have never allowed myself to get into a quarrel or an altercation with him, as the archbishop [of Capua, Nicolas von Schönberg] seems to hint. . . .

A little while ago at Augsburg they were selling Luther's picture with a halo; it was offered without a halo for sale here, and all the copies were disposed of in a trice before I could get one. Yesterday I saw on one and the same page, Luther with a book and Hutten with a sword. Over them was printed in fair letters: 'To the Champions of Christian Freedom, M. Luther and Ulrich von Hutten.' Each was praised in a tetrastich beneath; Hutten was threatening with his sword, according to the poet. A nobleman showed me such a picture, but I have not been able to get another. So far has the world gone that the Germans in blind adoration press around these two scoundrels, and adore even during their lifetime the men who were bold enough to cause a schism, whose words they oppose to the love of neighbour and the command of the Gospel in order to tear the seamless coat of Christ. And I am given up to such people! . . .

WORMS

Smith, *Correspondence*, I, 454 *et seq.*

5 Aleander to the Vice-chancellor Cardinal de Medici at Rome, 17 April 1521

This morning early I had a talk with the confessor in order to give the necessary directions for our plan. Then in the palace where they had as yet come to no decision on any question, I arranged that the electors should be summoned before the emperor at about two o'clock in the afternoon, and the other princes and estates at four, and that then Luther should appear simply to answer the questions put him and not to be heard further. I myself made the necessary arrangements, without however having our names appear, for we have always acted according to the wording of the Bull, both because there is no other way for us to act and because this is the best for attaining our end.

An immense crowd greeted the appearance of the arch-heretic, who was questioned before the emperor, princes and estates, in the name of the emperor and realm, as follows. Chance entrusted the duty of questioning him to the official of Trier, a learned and orthodox man, who is very conscientious in carrying out the apostolic and imperial mandates. In Trier he burned the heretical books so thoroughly that not one was left. This truly excellent man, for whom God be praised, lives in the same house with me, in the very next room.

He spoke to Luther as follows: 'Martin Luther, the emperor and realm have summoned you hither, that you may say and tell them whether you have composed these books,' for at the emperor's orders I had sent in twenty-five or more Lutheran books, 'and others which bear your name, and, secondly, that you may let us know whether you propose to defend and stand by these books.' Then the titles of the works were read one after another.

Then Luther answered first that all the books were his, and that he recognized them for his own. (This was a lie, for everyone knows that some of the books have other authors, although they go under Martin's name.) To the second question he said, that as it was the most difficult question in the world, concerning the faith, he must pray for time to consider his answer. Then the emperor with his privy council went apart, as did the electors in their own body, and the other princes and the representatives of the cities.

After due deliberation, the said official again spoke in the name of the Empire and the realm to this effect: That as Luther had previously been summoned by the realm, and the reason of his citation communicated to him, they were naturally much surprised that he did not have his answer ready on his arrival. Also that they were under no obligation to grant a respite in questions of faith, as this could only be done with danger and scandal to believers. (Would to God they had acted on this principle five months ago, as they should have.) Nevertheless, he continued, of the pure mercy and grace of the Emperor a respite was granted him until four o'clock tomorrow. Then the emperor had the official say to him that he should consider well that he had written against his Holiness and the See of St. Peter, and that he had sown many heresies – for they called things by their right names as was good – from which such scandal had arisen that unless preventive measures were immediately taken, it would kindle a conflagration which neither Luther's recantation nor the imperial power could quench. Therefore they admonished him to change his attitude. Then he was dismissed without speaking further. The fool entered smiling and, before the emperor, kept his head turning continually hither and thither; but when he left he did not seem so cheerful. Many even of his supporters after they had seen him said that he was foolish; others that he was possessed. But many others thought him a pious man, full of the Holy Ghost. In any case he has lost considerable reputation in the regard of all.

WORMS

Smith, *Correspondence*, I, 525 *et seq.*

I   THE DIET OF WORMS, APRIL 1521

It looks as though, once the question was settled (despite Aleander's protest) that Luther should appear, the authorities wanted to settle the matter as swiftly and tidily as possible. Copies of his books were on a table. He would be formally asked if they were his and invited then and there to recant. But it did not pass off in this way. Luther's lawyer friend cried out 'Make them read the titles!' – and Luther himself seems to have surprised the company by asking for time to consider. That this was granted turned the tide. That night he wrote out a few notes, which have survived and which betray no agitation. The next day he suceeded in making a real speech – though an impromptu attack on Rome was promptly smothered – and in ending with a note of defiance which has run through centuries. The famous 'Here I stand. I can do no other' does not exist in the oldest, primary version, but as has so often been said, it is a true myth. What is sometimes overlooked is that he offered to recant if convinced by scripture and 'evident reason', an enigmatic phrase which deserves considera-tion. In the following days he was granted what he had long desired, a chance to confer with reputable and reasonably friendly theologians. But despite the new atmosphere, in which the Archbishop of Trier and the humanist lawyer Peutinger played leading roles, Luther could not be drawn at this stage and after so much deliberation into compromise, and the discussions broke down about the authority of Councils. Taking advantage of his safe-conduct, Luther now withdrew to be declared outlaw by the Edict of Worms which a rump diet now passed, in a document much influenced, if not composed, by the papal nuncio, Jerome Aleander.

1   Luther's Answer before the Emperor and the Diet of Worms, 18 April 1521

On the next day, the fifth of the Festival [*Misericordia Domini*], just after four p.m., the herald came and led Dr Martin to the imperial court. The princes were engaged, and he had to wait till six p.m. among a great crowd of people which by their very number wearied and fretted him. But when the assembly began and Martin stood forward, the official [Eck] broke out with these words:

'Yesterday evening His Imperial Majesty prescribed this hour for you, Martin Luther, when you had publicly acknowledged as your own the books which we yesterday read out by name. But when you were asked if you wished any of them to be withdrawn, or whether you stood by all that you had published, you asked for time to think it over. This time is now at an end – and indeed by rights you should not have been granted any more time for consideration, for you have known long enough why you have been summoned here.

'Indeed, every man ought to be sure enough about his religious beliefs to be able to give a confident and trustworthy account of them whenever it is demanded, especially a man like you – so great and so experienced a Professor of Theology. Come now: answer at last His Majesty's question – you have appreciated his kindness in obtaining for yourself time for reflection: do you wish to stand by the books recognized as yours? Or do you wish to retract anything?'

The official had spoken in Latin and German, and Dr Martin replied in the same two languages, speaking like a suppliant, yet without raising his voice – modestly, but with no lack of Christian warmth and firmness, which whetted their appetites for the speech of his antagonist and the sight of his own high spirit humbled. Above all they looked most eagerly for his revocation, some hope of which they had conceived from his request for time for deliberation. This is what he said:

'My lord, emperor most serene, princes most illustrious, lords most gracious, I am here obedient to the order made yesterday evening that I should appear at this time. By the mercy of God I beseech your most Serene Majesty and your most illustrious lordships to deign to hear with forbearance my cause – which (I hope) is both just and true. If through my inexperience I do not give any one his proper title, or offend in any way against courtly etiquette, I beg you of your kindness to pardon me as a man whose life has not been spent in the courts of princes but in the cells of monks, and who can testify of himself nothing more than that he has hitherto taught and written with a simplicity of

mind which looked solely to the glory of God and the sincere upbuild-
ing of Christian believers.

'Most serene emperor, most illustrious princes: two questions were
put to me yesterday by your Highness, whether I acknowledged as
mine a list of books published under my name, and whether I wished
to hold to my defence of them or to revoke them. I gave a deliberate
and plain answer to the first, and I stand by it and always shall –
namely, that the books were mine, being published by me under my
own name, unless perchance it has happened that by the guile or
meddlesome cleverness of my rivals things in them have been altered
or omitted. For I only acknowledge what is solely my own and what I
alone have written, and not the interpretations which the industry of
others has added.

'In answer to the second question, may I ask your Highness and your
lordships to deign to take note that my books are not all of the same
kind. In some I have dealt with religious faith and morals so simply and
evangelically that my very antagonists are compelled to confess that
these books are useful, harmless and fit to be read by Christians. Even
the Bull, savage and cruel as it is, grants that some of my books are
harmless, even though it condemns them by a judgement that is simply
monstrous. If, then, I were to start revoking them, what (I beg you)
should I be doing? Should I not alone of mankind be condemning that
very truth which friends and enemies alike confess? Should I not alone
be wrestling against the agreed confession of all?

'Another class of my writings consists of polemic against the Papacy
and the doctrine of the Papists, as men who by their most evil teachings
and examples have laid waste all Christendom, body and soul. Nobody
can deny or dissemble this: the experience and the complaint of all men
bear witness that by the laws of the Pope and man-made doctrines, the
consciences of the faithful have been most wretchedly ensnared, tormented, tortured; that above all, in this renowned German nation,
goods and wealth have been devoured by tyranny unbelievable, and to
this day the devouring goes on, endlessly and by most grievous means.
Yet the canon law of the Papists itself provides that Papal laws and
doctrines contrary to the Gospel or the opinions of the Fathers should
be counted erroneous and rejected. If, then, I revoke these books, all I
shall achieve is to add strength to tyranny, and open not the windows
but the doors to this monstrous godlessness, for a wider and freer range
than it has ever dared before. The memorial of my revocation would
be the kingdom of their wickedness, with licence complete and un-
bridled, exercising over its wretched subjects a sway by far the most

intolerable of all, and even strengthened and stabilised if word got abroad that I had revoked my books with the authority of your serene Majesty and all the Roman Empire. Good God, what wickedness and tyranny should I then let loose!

'A third class of my writings has been aimed at certain private persons and (as they say) people of consequence, who have laboured to defend the Roman tyranny and undermine my religious teaching. Here I confess I have been more acrimonious than befits my religion or my calling. For I do not pose as a saint, and I am not disputing about my own life but about the teaching of Christ. Yet the way is not clear for me to revoke even these writings, for by such revocation I should lend my countenance to the reign of tyranny and wickedness, which would hold more savage and violent sway than ever among the people of God.

'However, because I am a man and not God, I can bring no other protection to my writings than my Lord Jesus Christ brought to his own teaching, when at the interrogation before Annas he was struck by a servant and said: "If I have spoken evil, testify to the evil." If the Lord himself, who knew he could not err, did not disdain to listen to testimony against his teaching, even from the meanest of slaves, how much more should I, the dregs of a man, who cannot but err, seek and await for someone to bear witness against my teaching? I therefore beg by the mercy of God that your serene Majesty, your illustrious lordships, or anyone at all, from the highest to the lowest, who is able, should bear witness, convict me of error, vanquish me by the prophets or the evangelists of scripture. I shall be only too ready, if I am convinced, to revoke any error, and in that case I shall be the first to cast my books into the fire. . . .'

To these words the imperial orator replied in tones of reproach that Luther's answer was not to the point; it was not for Luther to call in question things which had once been condemned or defined by Church councils. He therefore demanded a simple answer with no strings attached: would Luther revoke or would he not?

Luther replied: 'Since your serene Majesty and your lordships request a simple answer, I shall give it, with no strings and no catches. Unless I am convicted by the testimony of scripture or plain reason (for I believe neither in Pope nor councils alone, since it is agreed that they have often erred and contradicted themselves), I am bound by the scriptures I have quoted, and my conscience is captive to the Word of God. I neither can nor will revoke anything, for it is neither safe nor honest to act against one's conscience. Amen.'

Latin in Kidd, Doc. 42*

2   The Edict of Worms, May 1521

Charles V, . . . emperor . . . , to the electors, princes etc., one and all, greetings and blessings. . . .

§4   . . . None of you can be in any doubt how far the errors and heresies which a certain Martin Luther, of the Augustinian order, seeks to disseminate, depart from the Christian way. . . .

§25   . . . hence it is our duty to proceed against this festering disease as follows:

§26   First: to the praise and glory of Almighty God and the defence of the Christian faith and the honour due to the Pontiff and See of Rome – and furthermore with the unanimous agreement and wish of our own and the Holy Empire's electors, princes and orders now gathered in this place – we pronounce and declare that the said Martin Luther shall be held in detestation by us and each and all of you as a limb severed from the Church of God, the author of a pernicious schism, a manifest and obstinate heretic; and this we do in order that the whole business may never be forgotten, and that the decree, sentence and condemnation in the Bull, which our Holy Father the Pope issued in his capacity as Judge Ordinary of religious controversies, may be put into effect. It is our will that this should be publicized by these presents, in which our edicts and demands are made to each and all of you, under the engagement and oath which bind you to us and the Holy Empire, to the end that you should keep clear of the charge of treason and of consequent proscription and excommunication pronounced by us and the Empire. . . .

§27   Our strict order . . . is that after the appointed twenty days which terminate on the 14th of this month of May, you shall refuse the aforesaid Martin Luther hospitality, lodging and bed; that none shall feed and nourish him with food or drink, or assist and further him by the counsel and help of word or deed, secretly or openly; but wherever you meet him, if you have sufficient force, you shall take him prisoner and deliver him (or cause him to be delivered) to us in close custody, or at least send us information where he may be captured. . . .

§28   As for his friends, adherents, enthusiasts, patrons, supporters, partisans, sympathisers, rivals, imitators, with their property – personal or real: . . . we order that you shall attack, overthrow, seize and wrest their property from them, taking it all into your own possession. Nobody shall hinder you or stand in your way, unless the owner offers convincing evidence and proof that he has abandoned this dangerous way and obtained Papal absolution.

§29 As for the books of Martin Luther which our Holy Father the Pope has condemned, as well as any of his many other writings, in German or Latin, . . . we order that nobody shall henceforth dare to buy, sell, keep, copy, print or cause them to be copied and printed, or approve his opinions, or support, preach, defend or assert them in any way. . . . For they are impious, foul, suspect, half-baked [*diluta*], the work of a notorious and persistent heretic.

§31 We decree that . . . all in authority . . . and especially magistrates . . . here and throughout the Empire . . . shall under severe orders and penalties . . . ensure that . . . the works of Luther . . . are burned, and by this and other means utterly destroyed. . . .

§37 Finally, to forestall occasions of future heresies . . . we draw on our imperial and royal prerogative, as well as the deliberate and unanimous consent of our own and the imperial electors and orders, . . . and decree that no man, printer or otherwise, shall himself publish any book, or re-issue any publication of others, in which any mention of the Christian faith is made, unless the local Ordinary has been informed and approves of it . . . and the permission of the Theological Faculty of some University has been obtained. . . .

Latin in Kidd, Doc. 45*

J   LUTHER'S CONDEMNATION AND EXCOMMUNICATION

In a lecture to the first International Congress of Luther Studies at Aarhus, 1958, R. H. Bainton raised some interesting questions about Luther's condemnation by the Church authorities. The initial Bull *Exsurge Domine* gave Luther sixty days in which to recant. But if he did not, was he then automatically excommunicated? The fact that a further Bull, *Decet Romanum* followed on 3 January 1521 would seem to imply that he was not. Aleander had apparently not received copies of the second Bull on the 29 April 1521, though it had arrived by 8 May. In other words, Luther was condemned by the temporal powers, by the emperor at the Diet of Worms and in the Edict of Worms which followed, before he had been formally excommunicated by the Church. Of course, the temporal authorities knew about both Bulls, but the second had certainly not been published. Bainton maintains therefore that Aleander in impatience and almost in despair was prepared to treat the imperial Diet as an authoritative Church council, despite its lay character, in order to get Luther effectively condemned, though he had done his best to prevent Luther being called to the Diet in the first place, on the grounds that Luther had already been condemned by the Church. The fact that Aleander did absent himself from the fateful appearance of Luther at the Diet suggests that Bainton's case is not unanswerable.

1   The Bull 'Decet Romanum': the Condemnation and Excommunication of Martin Luther, the Heretic, and his Followers, January 1521

The Bull *Exsurge Domine* (**G, 2**) is easily available (e.g. Kidd, Doc. 38), and we have printed only extracts here. But *Decet Romanum*, the real and effective excommunication, with its extremely awkward implications for Frederick the Wise as Luther's patron and for all Luther's friends, we now print in full. It is a rare document which has almost disappeared from view.

Preamble

Through the power given him from God, the Roman Pontiff has been appointed to administer spiritual and temporal punishments as each case severally deserves. The purpose of this is the repression of the wicked designs of misguided men, who have been so captivated by the debased impulse of their evil purposes as to forget the fear of the Lord, to set aside with contempt canonical decrees and apostolic commandments, and to dare to formulate new and false dogmas and to introduce the evil of schism into the Church of God – or to support, help and adhere to such schismatics, who make it their business to cleave asunder the seamless robe of our Redeemer and the unity of the orthodox faith. Hence it befits the Pontiff, lest the vessel of Peter appear to sail without pilot or oarsman, to take severe measures against such men and their followers, and by multiplying punitive measures and by other suitable remedies to see to it that these same overbearing men, devoted as they are to purposes of evil, along with their adherents, should not deceive the multitude of the simple by their lies and their deceitful devices, nor drag them along to share their own error and ruination, contaminating them with what amounts to a contagious disease. It also befits the Pontiff, having condemned the schismatics, to ensure their still greater confounding by publicly showing and openly declaring to all faithful

Christians how formidable are the censures and punishments to which such guilt can lead; to the end that by such public declaration they themselves may return, in confusion and remorse, to their true selves, making an unqualified withdrawal from the prohibited conversation, fellowship and (above all) obedience to such accursed excommunicates; by this means they may escape divine vengeance and any degree of participation in their damnation.

§1   [Here the Pope recounts his previous Bull *Exsurge Domine* (**G, 2**) and continues]

§2   We have been informed that after this previous missive had been exhibited in public and the interval or intervals it prescribed had elapsed – and we hereby give solemn notice to all faithful Christians that these intervals have and are elapsed – many of those who had followed the errors of Martin took cognisance of our missive and its warnings and injunctions; the spirit of a saner counsel brought them back to themselves, they confessed their errors and abjured the heresy at our instance, and by returning to the true Catholic faith obtained the blessing of absolution with which the self-same messengers had been empowered; and in several states and localities of the said Germany the books and writings of the said Martin were publicly burned, as we had enjoined.

Nevertheless Martin himself – and it gives us grievous sorrow and perplexity to say this – the slave of a depraved mind, has scorned to revoke his errors within the prescribed interval and to send us word of such revocation, or to come to us himself; nay, like a stone of stumbling, he has feared not to write and preach worse things than before against us and this Holy See and the Catholic faith, and to lead others on to do the same.

He has now been declared a heretic; and so also others, whatever their authority and rank, who have recked nought of their own salvation but publicly and in all men's eyes become followers of Martin's pernicious and heretical sect, and given him openly and publicly their help, counsel and favour, encouraging him in their midst in his disobedience and obstinacy, or hindering the publication of our said missive: such men have incurred the punishments set out in that missive, and are to be treated rightfully as heretics and avoided by all faithful Christians, as the Apostle says [*Titus* III: 10-11].

§3   Our purpose is that such men should rightfully be ranked with Martin and other accursed heretics and excommunicates, and that even as they have ranged themselves with the obstinacy in sinning of the said Martin, they shall likewise share his punishments and his name, by bearing with them everywhere the title 'Lutheran' and the punishments it incurs.

Our previous instructions were so clear and so effectively publicized and we shall adhere so strictly to our present decrees and declarations, that they will lack no proof, warning or citation.

Our decrees which follow are passed against Martin and others who follow him in the obstinacy of his depraved and damnable purpose, as also against those who defend and protect him with a military bodyguard, and do not fear to support him with their own resources or in any other way, and have and do presume to offer and afford help, counsel and favour toward him. All their names, surnames and rank – however lofty and dazzling their dignity may be – we wish to be taken as included in these decrees with the same effect as if they were individually listed and could be so listed in their publication, which must be furthered with an energy to match their contents.

On all these we decree the sentences of excommunication, of anathema, of our perpetual condemnation and interdict; of privation of dignities, honours and property on them and their descendants, and of declared unfitness for such possessions; of the confiscation of their goods and of the crime of treason; and these and the other sentences, censures and punishments which are inflicted by canon law on heretics and are set out in our aforesaid missive, we decree to have fallen on all these men to their damnation.

§4 We add to our present declaration, by our Apostolic authority, that states, territories, camps, towns and places in which these men have temporarily lived or chanced to visit, along with their possessions – cities which house cathedrals and metropolitans, monasteries and other religious and sacred places, privileged or unprivileged – one and all are placed under our ecclesiastical interdict. While this interdict lasts, no pretext of Apostolic Indulgence (except in cases the law allows, and even there as it were with the doors shut and those under excommunication and interdict excluded) shall avail to allow the celebration of mass and the other divine offices. We prescribe and enjoin that the men in question are everywhere to be denounced publicly as excommunicated, accursed, condemned, interdicted, deprived of possessions and incapable of owning them. They are to be strictly shunned by all faithful Christians.

§5 We would make known to all the small store that Martin, his followers and the other rebels have set on God and his Church by their obstinate and shameless temerity. We would protect the herd from one infectious animal, lest its infection spread to the healthy ones. Hence we lay the following injunction on each and every patriarch, archbishop, bishop, on the prelates of patriarchal, metropolitan, cathedral and collegiate churches, and on the religious of every Order – even the mendicants – privileged or unprivileged, wherever they may be stationed: that in the strength of their vow of obedience and on pain of the sentence of excommunication, they shall, if so required in the execution of these presents, publicly announce and cause to be announced by others in their churches, that this same Martin and the rest are excommunicate, accursed, condemned, heretics, hardened, interdicted, deprived of possessions and incapable of owning them, and so listed in the enforcement of these presents. Three days will be given: we pronounce canonical warning and allow one day's notice on the first, another on the second, but on the third peremptory and final execution of our order. This shall take place on a Sunday or some other festival, when a large congregation assembles for worship. The banner of the cross shall be raised, the bells rung, the candles lit and after a time extinguished, cast on the ground and trampled under foot, and the stones shall be cast forth three times, and the other ceremonies observed which are usual in such cases. The faithful Christians, one and all, shall be enjoined strictly to shun these men.

We would occasion still greater confounding on the said Martin and the other heretics we have mentioned, and on their adherents, followers and partisans: hence, on the strength of their vow of obedience we enjoin each and every patriarch, archbishop and all other prelates, that even as they were appointed on the authority of Jerome to allay schisms, so now in the present crisis, as their office obliges them, they shall make themselves a wall of defence for their Christian people. They shall not keep silence like dumb dogs that cannot bark, but incessantly cry and lift up their voice, preaching and causing to be preached the word of God and the truth of the Catholic faith against the damnable articles and heretics aforesaid.

§6   To each and every rector of the parish churches, to the rectors of all the Orders, even the mendicants, privileged or unprivileged, we enjoin in the same terms, on the strength of their vow of obedience, that appointed by the Lord as they are to be like clouds, they shall sprinkle spiritual showers on the people of God, and have no fear in giving the widest publicity to the condemnation of the aforesaid articles, as their office obliges them. It is written that perfect love casteth out fear. Let each and every one of you take up the burden of such a meritorious duty with complete devotion; show yourselves so punctilious in its execution, so zealous and eager in word and deed, that from your labours, by the favour of divine grace, the hoped-for harvest will come in, and that through your devotion you will not only earn that crown of glory which is the due recompense of all who promote religious causes, but also attain from us and the said Holy See the unbounded commendation that your proved diligence will deserve.

§7 However, since it would be difficult to deliver the present missive, with its declarations and announcements, to Martin and the other declared excommunicates in person, because of the strength of their faction, our wish is that the public nailing of this missive on the doors of two cathedrals – either both metropolitan, or one cathedral and one metropolitan of the churches in the said Germany – by a messenger of ours in those places, shall have such binding force that Martin and the others we have declared shall be shown to be condemned at every point as decisively as if the missive had been personally made known and presented to them.

§8 It would also be difficult to transmit this missive to every single place where its publication might be necessary. Hence our wish and authoritative decree is that copies of it, sealed by some ecclesiastical prelate or by one of our aforesaid messengers, and countersigned by the hand of some public notary, should everywhere bear the same authority as the production and exhibition of the original itself.

§9 No obstacle is afforded to our wishes by the Apostolic constitutions and orders, or by anything in our aforesaid earlier missive which we do not wish to stand in the way, or by any other pronouncements to the contrary.

§10 No one whatsoever may infringe this our written decision, declaration, precept, injunction, assignation, will, decree; or rashly contravene it. Should anyone dare to attempt such a thing, let him know that he will incur the wrath of Almighty God and of the blessed Apostles Peter and Paul.

Written at St. Peter's, Rome, on the third of January 1521, during the eighth year of our pontificate.

Bullarum . . . Taurinensis Editio, Seb. Franco et Henrico Dalmazzo Editoribus (Turin, 1860), v, 761 *et seq.*★

2   To Spalatin, 14 May 1521: the Aftermath of Worms and Luther's 'Kidnapping'

In the light of Luther's double condemnation as heretic and outlaw, by Church and Empire, his friends were now explicitly entangled in danger, since *Decet Romanum* applied the same penalties to those who befriended and supported him. There was only one thing to do, if Frederick the Wise were not to abandon Luther to his enemies, something he had long refused to do, and which was indeed to his honour, unthinkable. Luther must disappear. The arranged kidnapping was the consequence, though to the world at large it seemed that Luther might have been done away with by his enemies, and it was indeed weeks and months before the secret leaked out.

To his dearest friend in Christ, George Spalatin, a most faithful servant of Christ at Aldeburg. . . .

Greetings. . . . I have purposely not written you before, for fear that the recent rumour of my capture might cause someone to intercept my letters. Various stories are told about me here; but the prevalent idea is that I have been captured by friends sent from Franconia. To-morrow my imperial safe-conduct expires. I am grieved to read in your letter that, armed with such a harsh edict, their savagery will hunt out even people's consciences; my grief is not on my own account, but on theirs – for the evil they will call down on their own heads through their folly, and the great hatred with which they are going to load themselves. What dreadful hostility such shameless violence will incite! But let be: the time of their visitation is perchance at hand. . . .

As for me, I sit here all day long, at ease with my wine. I am reading the Bible in Greek and Hebrew. I shall write a sermon in German on the freedom of auricular confession; I shall continue my work on the *Psalms* and the *Postillae* as soon as I have received what I need from Wittenberg, including the unfinished *Magnificat*.

You would not believe with what kindness the Abbot of Hersfeld received us. He sent the chancellor and the treasurer a good mile out to meet us; then he himself met us with many horsemen at his castle and escorted us into the town. The council welcomed us inside the gates. In his monastery he fed us royally, and made over his own bed for my use. On the fifth morning they made me preach. It was no use my pleading that they might lose their royal privileges if the emperor's officers should proceed to interpret this as a breach of the promise I had given, since they had forbidden me to preach en route – although I maintained that I had not consented that the Word of God should be fettered (which is true). I also preached at Eisenach, but the timid incumbent protested before me in the presence of a notary and witnesses, although he humbly apologised for having to do this through fear of his tyrants. . . .

The abbot attended us on the next day as far as the forest; the chancellor joined us, and the abbot fed us all again at Berka. In the end we were met by the people of Eisenach who came out to meet us on foot, and we entered Eisenach in the evening. Next morning all my companions left, including Jerome [Schürpf]. I went on through the forest to my kith and kin (who occupy almost all that neighbourhood). I left them, and when we turned towards Walterhausen, a little later – near to Altenstein Castle – I was captured. Amsdorf had of course to know that I was going to be captured by someone, but he does not know where I am being held.

My brother-friar, seeing the horsemen in time, jumped off the cart, and they say that he reached Walterhausen unobserved in the evening, on foot.

Here I was stripped of my own clothes and clad in those of a knight. I am letting my hair and my beard grow, and you would hardly know me – indeed, for some time I haven't recognized myself! I am now living in Christian freedom, exempt from all the laws of that tyrant – although I could have preferred that the Swine of Dresden [Duke George of Saxony] had been capable of killing me when I was preaching in public, had it pleased God that I should suffer for his Word. God's will be done. Farewell, and pray for me. Salute 'your whole court'.

WARTBURG   MARTIN LUTHER
                              Latin in *W.A.*, *Br.W.*, II, 336 *et seq.**

K LUTHER'S 'CAPTIVITY'

That Luther was a prisoner in safe and friendly captivity was a closely guarded secret. Meanwhile rumours circulated. The great painter Albrecht Dürer confided to his diary, his fears that Luther had been murdered and lamented 'O God, if Luther be dead who will proclaim the holy Gospel so clearly to us? O good Christians help me earnestly to lament this inspired man of God and pray that he will send another.' On the Wartburg, Luther learned to his horror that Albert of Mainz was preparing to authorize new Indulgences, and wrote a vehement protest threatening to expose Albert: the consequence was a letter, mealy-mouthed in contrition, from Albert through his secretary Wolfgang Capito, the future reformer of Strasbourg.

1 To Albert, Archbishop and Elector of Mainz, 1 December 1521

... Your Grace has again erected at Halle that idol which robs poor simple Christians of their money and their souls. You have thus shown that the criminal blunder for which Tetzel was blamed was not due to him alone, but also to the Archbishop of Mainz, who, not regarding my gentleness to him, insists on taking all the blame on himself. Perhaps your Grace thinks I am no more to be reckoned with, but am looking out for my own safety, and that his Imperial Majesty has extinguished the poor monk. On the contrary, I wish your Grace to know that I will do what Christian love demands without fearing the gates of hell, much less unlearned popes, bishops, and cardinals. I will not suffer it nor keep silence when the Archbishop of Mainz gives out that it is none of his business to give information to a poor man who asks for it. The truth is that your ignorance is wilful, as long as the thing ignored brings you in money. I am not to blame, but your own conduct. . . .

Wherefore I write to tell your Grace that if the idol is not taken down, my duty to godly doctrine and Christian salvation will absolutely force me to attack your Grace publicly as I did the Pope, and oppose your undertaking, and lay all the odium which Tetzel once had on the Archbishop of Mainz, and show all the world the difference between a bishop and a wolf. . . .

I beg and expect a right speedy answer from your Grace within the next fortnight, for at the expiration of that time my pamphlet against the Idol of Halle will be published unless a proper answer comes. And if this letter is received by your Grace's secretaries and does not come into your own hands, I will not hold off for that reason. Secretaries should be true and a bishop should so order his court that that reaches him which should reach him. God give your Grace his grace unto a right mind and will.

Your Grace's obedient, humble servant,

WARTBURG   MARTIN LUTHER

Smith, *Life and Letters,* 127 *et seq.*

L   LUTHER'S HEALTH AND WRITINGS: THE ZWICKAU PROPHETS

On the Wartburg, Luther soon found the lonely, sedentary life a great trial. He was beset by *Anfechtungen* – his word for 'temptations'. His spirit, now flung back on itself after the long ordeal of the past months, became a prey to doubts and despondencies. His body, having to cope with an unwontedly rich diet, and with lack of exercise, began to play up, and constipation and piles were the result. Meanwhile, in Wittenberg a new and dangerous ferment had arisen. In the autumn of 1521 the Reformation in Wittenberg itself took a more drastic turn, and by the end of the year Luther's senior colleague Andrew Karlstadt had taken the lead, seconded by a fiery Augustinian, Gabriel Zwilling, in a programme of violent and radical reform. Luther's own friends, Melanchthon and Justus Jonas were to some extent caught up in the new current, but unable to supply the kind of moderate leadership now needed if the Reformation were not to get altogether out of hand. There were ominous student riots and an outbreak of image-breaking. It was at this moment, Christmas time 1521, that there arrived the radical 'Zwickau prophets' who had been expelled from Zwickau, where Thomas Müntzer had been their colleague and leader.

Led by Nicholas Storch, a weaver, they brought novel doctrines, and spoke of heavenly visions and divine colloquies, basing their claim to inspiration on plausible and eloquent scriptural arguments. Melanchthon got rather the worse of a debate with one of them, Mark Stübner, an old pupil of his own, and wrote in some alarm and confusion for Luther's advice. Probably neither he nor Jonas could quite see, on Luther's own teaching, how these men could be refuted, and indeed how to deal with them at all. Luther's reply is interesting, full of common sense, and lays down rules for testing so called 'prophets' which he was to maintain in coming years, since the advent of the Zwickau prophets marks the opening of Luther's second Front, with Papists on the one hand and radicals on the other. The Zwickau prophets rejected infant baptism and Luther in this famous letter to Melanchthon puts forward his own (not entirely original) arguments in favour of the baptism of children.

Although separated from his books, Luther contrived to write notable works on the Wartburg. He arranged for publication his expositions of Gospels and Epistles, and penned one of his most powerful controversial pieces, *Contra Latomum*, in which he magisterially expounds the relation of justification by faith to the renewing power of the Holy Spirit. And he began his greatest project and most genial achievement, the translation of the New Testament.

1   To Melanchthon, 13 July 1521

Your letter displeased me for two reasons: first, you carry your cross too impatiently – you give in too much to your feelings, and your nature (as always) is too gentle. Secondly, you praise me too highly; you are dreadfully wrong in making so much of me, as if I was concerned in the same degree for the cause of God. This high opinion you have of me puts me to shame and tortures me, when in fact I sit here at ease, hardened and unfeeling – alas! praying little, grieving little for the Church of God, burning rather in the fierce fires of my untamed flesh. It comes to this: I *should* be afire in the spirit; in reality I am afire in the flesh, with lust, laziness, idleness, sleepiness. It is perhaps because you have all ceased praying for me that God has turned away from me; you, Philip, are already taking my place, and God's gifts have given you more authority and appeal than I had.

For the last eight days I have written nothing, nor prayed nor studied,

partly from self-indulgence, partly from another vexatious handicap.[1]
If the latter does not improve, I shall go straight to Erfurt and drop my
incognito, and we shall see each other there, for I shall be consulting the
doctors or the surgeons. For I really cannot stand it any longer; I could
more easily suffer ten big wounds than this small symptom of a lesion.
Possibly the Lord afflicts me in this way in order to force me out of this
retreat back into the public eye. . . .

   Pray for me, I beg you, for in my seclusion here I am submerged in
sins. . . .

MARTIN LUTHER
Hermit

WARTBURG

Latin in *W.A., Br.W.,* II, 356 *et seq.*★

2   To Melanchthon, 1 August 1521

. . . If you are a preacher of grace, then preach grace that is true and
not fictitious; if grace is true, you must bear a true and not a fictitious
sin. God does not save fictitious sinners. Be a sinner and sin boldly (*esto
peccator et pecca fortiter*),[2] but have faith and rejoice in Christ more
boldly still, for he is the victor over sin, death and the world. We *must*
sin as long as we are here; this life is not the dwelling-place of righteousness, but as Peter says [*II Peter* III:13] we look for new heavens and a
new earth, in which righteousness dwells. It suffices that through the
riches of God's glory we have come to know the Lamb that takes away
the sin of the world; sin will not tear us away from him, even though
we commit fornication and murder thousands and thousands of times
in one day. Do you think that the price that was paid for the redemption
of our sins by so great and such a Lamb was so small [that sin could tear
us away from him]?

Latin in *W.A., Br.W.,* II, 373★

3   To Spalatin, 15 August 1521

. . . Last Monday I went hunting for a couple of days to see what that
'bitter-sweet' pleasure of heroes is like. We caught two hares and a few
poor partridges – a worthy occupation for men with nothing to do!

---

[1] *partim tentationibus carnis, partim alia molestia vexatus.* The *alia molestia* is his constipation; the *tentationes carnis* are the 'lust, laziness' etc. of the previous paragraph. This is a
good example of Luther's metaphorical use of *caro* in the pejorative Pauline sense.

[2] This *pecca fortiter* passage should be read in its context. To ignore the rhetorical figure
is as ruinous as it would be further on, where the rather difficult possibility of 'committing
fornication and murder thousands and thousands of times in one day' is contemplated.
The real emphasis is of course on the redeeming righteousness of Christ (*cf.* **C, 2**).

I theologized even among the snares and the dogs: the pleasure that this spectacle afforded was balanced by the mystery of the misery and pain it also inflicted. It was nothing else than an image of the devil hunting innocent little creatures with his ambushes and his hounds – those ungodly teachers the bishops and the theologians. I was only too conscious of this tragic image of simple and faithful souls. A still more dreadful image followed, when at my insistence we had saved alive a little rabbit. I had rolled it up into the sleeve of my cloak. I moved away some distance, and meanwhile the dogs found the poor creature, bit through the cloak, broke its right leg, choked it and killed it. Even such is the fury of the Pope and of Satan, raging to destroy even the souls that have been saved, and heeding nought of my efforts. I have had a surfeit of this kind of hunting. I prefer the more agreeable kind in which bears, wolves, boars, foxes – and all that breed of godless teachers – are pierced with spears and arrows.

Yet it consoles me that here to hand is an allegory of *salvation*. Hares and innocent creatures are captured by *men*, not by bears, wolves, hawks of prey and suchlike Bishops and theologians; to be swallowed up by the latter means hell, but by the former heaven!

I'm writing all this with my tongue in my cheek – don't miss the point that you courtiers, so keen on the chase, will yourselves be wild beasts in paradise, and even Christ, the supreme hunter, will have his hands full to catch and save you! While you are playing around hunting, you are being made game of yourselves. . . .

WARTBURG

Latin in *W.A.*, *Br.W.*, II, 380 *et seq.*★

4   To John Lang, Augustinian, 18 December 1521

. . . I shall remain here in seclusion till Easter, and write postils, and translate the New Testament into German, which so many people are anxious to have. I hear you also are occupied therewith. Go on with what you have begun. Would to God that every town had its interpreter, and that this book could be had in every language, and dwell in the hearts and hands of all. You will get all the rest of the news from the Wittenbergers. I am, God be praised, sound in body and well cared for, but much tried by sins and temptations. Pray for me, and go on prospering. From the wilderness.

MARTIN LUTHER
Currie, p. 94

5   To Melanchthon, 13 January 1522

To Philip Melanchthon, Christ's servant and faithful steward, my brother

. . . Now let me deal with the 'prophets'. Before I say anything else, I do not approve of your timidity, since you are stronger in spirit and learning than I. First of all, since they bear witness to themselves, one need not immediately accept them; according to John's counsel, the spirits are to be tested. If you cannot test them, then you have the advice of Gamaliel that you postpone judgement. Thus far I hear of nothing said or done by them that Satan could not also do or imitate. Yet find out for me whether they can prove [that they are called by God], for God has never sent anyone, not even the Son himself, unless he was called through men or attested by signs. In the old days the prophets had their authority from the law and the prophetic order, as we now receive authority through men. I definitely do not want the 'prophets' to be accepted if they state that they were called by mere revelation, since God did not even wish to speak to Samuel except through the authority and knowledge of Eli. This is the first thing that belongs to teaching in public.

In order to explore their individual spirit, too, you should inquire whether they have experienced spiritual distress and the divine birth, death and hell. If you should hear that all [their experiences] are pleasant, quiet, devout [as they say], and spiritual, then don't approve of them, even if they should say that they were caught up to the third heaven. The sign of the Son of Man is then missing, which is the only touchstone of Christians and a certain differentiator between the spirits. Do you want to know the place, time and manner of [true] conversations with God? Listen: 'Like a lion has he broken all my bones'; 'I am cast out from before your eyes'; 'My soul is filled with grief, and my life has approached hell.' The [Divine] Majesty [as they call it] does not speak in such a direct way to man that man could [actually] see it; but rather, 'Man shall not see me and live'. [Our] nature cannot bear even a small glimmer of God's [direct] speaking. As a result God speaks through men [indirectly], because not all can endure his speaking. The angel frightened even the Virgin, and also Daniel. And Jeremiah pleads, 'Correct me [O Lord] but in just measure', and, 'Be not a terror to me.' Why should I say more? As if the [Divine] Majesty could speak familiarly with the Old Adam without first killing him and drying him out so that his horrible stench would not be so foul, since God is a consuming fire! The dreams and visions of the saints are horrifying, too, at least after they are understood. Therefore examine [them] and do not even listen if they speak of the glorified Jesus, unless you have first heard of the crucified Jesus.

You will say, what does this have to do with the case? After all, it only refutes others, and does not establish our position. But how can I speak of our position when I am absent and do not know what they may present against it? If they do not appeal to anything but this passage, 'He who believeth and is baptized shall be saved', and to the fact that children cannot believe on their own account, that does not disturb me at all. For how will these prophets prove that children do not believe? Perhaps by the fact that children do not speak and express their faith. Fine! On that basis [we have to ask] how many hours [of the day] even we are Christians, in view of the fact that we sleep and do other things? Can't God in the same way keep faith in small children during the whole time of their infancy, as if it were a continuous sleep? Fine, you say. This confutes the opponents in the question concerning faith already infused. It is enough for now that they are shown to be the kind of people who can prove nothing and are moved by a false spirit.

What do you say concerning faith which is to be infused? [Here] nothing else is left but intrinsic faith; if we cannot uphold this, then there is nothing else to be debated, and baptism of small children simply has to be rejected.

You say, aren't the examples for extrinsic faith weak? I reply that there is nothing stronger. These 'prophets', or all the devils, should show one weak example of extrinsic faith! You quote the passage where Samuel prays for Saul, but this has nothing to do with it. Samuel grieved for Saul, he did not pray [for him]; or if he prayed, he did not pray in faith, that is, he did not believe he would obtain that for which he was praying but placed the outcome [of his prayer] in doubt and left it to the arbitrariness of God. It was the same as when David prayed for his little son, or when many other people pray for many other things. If he had been certain he would receive, he surely would have, because the promise of Christ in *Matthew* XXI [:22] stands fast, 'Whatever you may ask for, believe that you will receive it and you shall receive it.' And in *Matthew* XVII [:19], 'If two on earth', etc. This fact cannot be shaken: it is impossible that that for which one prays will not happen if one believes that it will happen. Otherwise the whole doctrine of faith would waver, and personal faith, which is based on [Christ's] promise, would be of no value. Indeed [the faith in which my neighbour intercedes on my behalf] belongs to me personally but is really also someone else's faith, so far as my neighbour is concerned; nevertheless it is necessary that [that for which the neighbour intercedes] in faith should happen in him [on whose behalf the neighbour makes the intercession]. All the examples from the Gospel pertain to this. For Christ has never rejected a single man who was brought to him through someone else's faith, but accepted all. What more should I say? The testimonies and examples of the whole scripture are on the side of extrinsic faith, that is, on the side of personal faith, which attains faith and whatever is desired for someone else.

Now one point remains unresolved, which is whether the Church believes faith is infused into infants. This question might perhaps arise in connection with the discussion of the [nature of the] Church, rather than of extrinsic faith and its efficaciousness. What extrinsic faith is able to do is not subject to discussion, since all things are possible to him who believes. [The question of the Church], however, is one of reality and not of theory. We cannot debate whether the Church has to believe that faith is infused into infants, since the Church has the authority not to baptize infants at all, nor is there any scripture passage which could force the Church to believe this, as there are Bible passages for other tenets.

What should we do here? Do we not approve of the theory? Who can see faith? Therefore we have to proceed to the [question of] the confession of faith, since confession for salvation is made with the mouth. What does the Church confess that it believes in this article? Is it not this, that children also participate in the benefits and promises of Christ? One may object here, however: what if Augustine and those whom you call the Church, or whom you believe are the Church, have erred at this point? Who will make us certain that the Church has to believe this, since we cannot prove it? This objection should be contradicted as follows: there may be no law, but there is the fact that this is believed in the Church. For who can be sure that Augustine believed in the Trinity if one does not trust his confession? I am certain that [Augustine's] confession agrees with scripture, but I do not know whether he believes what he confesses. But I see it as a special miracle of God that the article that infants are to be baptized is the only one which has never been denied, not even by heretics. No one's confession opposes it; on the contrary the constant and unanimous confession of the whole world supports this argument. To deny, however, that this is the confession of the true and legitimate Church, I consider tremendous ungodliness. This seems to me to be the same as if one were to deny the existence of the Church. If this were not so, no doubt the Church would have issued some contrary statement at least once, since the faith of the Church has never ceased, and since the Church was never without confession of its faith. You, as an understanding man, will deduce further conclusions from this.

To present a child for baptism is nothing else but to offer it to Christ, who is present on earth and opens [his] hands of grace [towards the child]; Christ has shown throughout his entire life that he accepts whoever is brought to him. Why should we then have any doubts at this point? This is one thing, at least, we have taken away from these 'prophets', namely, that they could prove their ideas, since they lack example and testimony; but we have both, and their testimony does not withstand ours. For who will argue this way: one has to believe and be baptized, therefore infants are not to be baptized? [The 'prophets'] certainly cannot draw this conclusion from this passage, since it does not prove that children do not believe. They presuppose this, and have to prove it on some other basis; but they are unable to do this. What is not against scripture is for scripture, and scripture is for it. On the basis of that same sophistry, they could also take away circumcision, saying: small children do not have Abraham's faith, therefore they should not have the sign of this same faith. We are certain that circumcision had the same power as baptism. Therefore I do not see why, only on the basis of God's authority and of this example, children shouldn't be baptized. There is only one difference: baptism is free and not compulsory like circumcision. It was therefore not necessary that baptism be bound to any certain times, ages, places, or other externals, since it is completely free in itself. Therefore what was then commanded to one people concerning the eighth day is now said to all people of every age: 'He who believes . . . ,' etc.

More on this when I see you. I have always expected Satan to touch this sore, but he did not want to do it through the Papists. It is among us and among our followers that he is stirring up this grievous schism, but Christ will quickly trample him under our feet.

I would also like to know how you understand that passage in *I Corinthians* VII [:14], 'Otherwise your children would be unclean, but now they are holy.' Do you want to have this understood only of adults, or of the sanctity of the flesh [in general]? I wish it would be demonstrated from this passage that according to apostolic custom, and in the time of the apostles, small children were baptized. Although I see what could be said concerning this sanctification, yet I would also like to have your opinion. Why should the Apostle [Paul] say this only of children, since all things are holy to the holy, and to the clean all things are clean?

Keep the little book against the [Arch]bishop of Mainz, so that it can go out [one day] and serve as a general censure, should others go insane like that. Please prepare a lodging for me, since the translation [of the Bible] will compel me to return to Wittenberg. Pray the Lord that this may be done in agreement with his will. I wish, however, to stay hidden as much as possible; meanwhile I shall proceed with what I have begun.

Farewell.

WARTBURG

Yours, MARTIN LUTHER
Amer. Edn., XLVIII, 365 *et seq.*

M   KARLSTADT AND WITTENBERG RADICALISM

Luther's theological principles, declared in his treatises, had profound practical implications, the ramifications of which touched social economic and political matters. In Wittenberg, from the beginning of October 1521, a movement began which became more and more radical, and was eventually led by Luther's senior colleague, Archdeacon of the Castle Church, Andrew Karlstadt, D.D., who introduced communion in both kinds, with a simplified liturgy, and who now championed a vernacular form of service. In addition, and theologically encouraged by Luther's *Monastic Vows* (1521) the Augustinians began to abandon the Wittenberg house, and their example was followed in Erfurt and elsewhere. Karlstadt then attacked pictures and images, and the result was a series of violent and anti-clerical protests by students and townsmen. In January 1522 the Wittenberg authorities drew up some reforming ordinances, regulating the social and economic effect of the changes, and setting up a common chest into which money from secularized church property might be put. All these changes greatly exercised the Elector Frederick, his chaplain and secretary Spalatin and their advisers, since the authorities of the Empire, meeting in Diet at Nuremberg, had forbidden any kind of religious innovation. Furthermore these disturbances might provide his jealous neighbour and kinsman, Duke George, with a pretext for military intervention and perhaps the dispossession of Frederick himself. In these circumstances Luther, against the advice of his prince, broke his hiding, returned to Wittenberg, and re-entering his pulpit in the parish church, dressed as an Augustinian hermit, delivered a series of sermons which effectively stemmed the incipient radical revolution. The 'stay-put' orders of the Elector were now effective, and Karlstadt discredited and in near disgrace. Wittenberg was saved for Luther's type of Reformation, but the revolutionary ferment went on in Thuringia, finding new centres in the preaching of John Strauss at Eisenach and Thomas Müntzer at Allstedt.

1 To the Elector Frederick of Saxony, 5 March 1522

Written in Borna on the way to Wittenberg, in answer to a letter from the Elector, which tried to dissuade Luther from coming.

To the serene high-born Prince Frederick, Elector of Saxony, etc. Grace and peace! Most gracious lord, Your Electoral Grace's writing and kind remembrance reached me on Friday evening, the night before I began my journey. That your Electoral Highness had the best intentions towards me is manifest. And this is my answer. Most gracious lord, I herewith desire to make it known that I have not received the Gospel from men, but from heaven, through our Lord Jesus Christ, so that I may well (which I shall henceforth do) glory in being able to style myself a servant and evangelist. That I desired to be cited before a human tribunal to have my cause tried was not because I had any doubts as to its truth, but solely because I wished to allure others. But now that I see my great humility only serves to abase the Gospel, and that Satan is ready to occupy the place I vacate, even if it be only by a hand-breadth, my conscience compels me to act differently. I have done sufficient for your Grace this year in remaining in my forced seclusion. For the devil knows it was not done out of fear. He saw into my heart, when I came into Worms, that although I had known there were as many devils ready to spring upon me as there were tiles on the house-roofs, I would joyfully have sprung into their midst.

Now Duke George is far from being equal to one devil, especially seeing the Father has, out of his loving-kindness, made us, through the Gospel, joyous lords over all the devils and death itself, and has permitted us to call him beloved Father. Your Grace can see for yourself that it would be the greatest insult one could pay to such a Father not to trust him entirely, showing that we are lords over Duke George's wrath. Were things in Leipzig as they are in Wittenberg, I would nevertheless ride in, even if it were to rain Duke Georges for nine days, and each was nine times more vehement than this one is. He looks upon my Lord Jesus as a man of straw. But I confess I have often wept and prayed for Duke George that God would enlighten him. And I shall once more weep and pray for him, and then never again.

And I beseech your Electoral Highness to help me to pray that we may be able to avert the judgement which is hanging over him continually.

I write all this to let your Grace see that I come to Wittenberg under higher protection than that of the Elector, and I have not the slightest intention of asking your Electoral Highness's help. For I consider I am more able to protect your Grace than you are to protect me; and, what is more, if I knew that your gracious Highness could and would protect me I would not come.

In this matter God alone must manage without any human intervention. Therefore he whose faith is greatest will receive the most protection. So, as I see your faith is very weak, I cannot regard you as the man who could either protect or save me. And seeing your Grace wishes to know how to act, as you seem to fancy you have done too little, I would respectfully inform you that you have already done too much, and must now do nothing at all. For God will not suffer your Electoral Highness's or my worrying and activities. He wishes it to be left to him, to him and no other, so let your Grace act accordingly.

If your Electoral Highness believes this, then he will be in security and peace; if not, I do and must allow your Electoral Grace to be tormented by care, which is the portion of all who do not believe.

Therefore, seeing I decline to follow your Grace, then you are innocent in God's sight if I am taken prisoner or killed. Your Electoral Highness shall henceforth act thus regarding your duty towards me as Elector. You must render obedience to the powers that be, and sustain the authority of His Imperial Majesty with all your might, as is only seemly for a member of the Empire, and not oppose the authorities in the event of their imprisoning or slaying me. For no one must oppose the authorities except He who has instituted them; for it is rebellion against God.

But I hope they will be sensible, and recognise that your Electoral Highness is born in a higher cradle, and should not be expected to wield the rod upon yourself.

If your Grace abide by the Electoral safe-conduct then you have done enough to show your obedience. For Christ has not taught me to be a Christian to the injury of others.

But should they command your Grace to lay hands on me yourself, then I shall say what to do.

I shall protect you from injury to body, soul and estate because of my affairs, whether your Grace believes it or not.

I herewith commit you to the mercy of God, and shall discuss things when necessary. I have written this hurriedly, so that your Grace may not be upset by my arrival; for I must rather be a comfort to every one than occasion of injury if I wish to be a true Christian.

I am dealing with a very different man from Duke George, with one who knows me well, and whom I do not know at all badly. Were your Grace only to believe he would see the glory of God, but as he has not yet believed, he has seen nothing. To God be love and praise to all eternity. Amen. Given at Borna by my escort. Your Electoral Grace's obedient servant,

BORNA

MARTIN LUTHER

Currie, 98 *et seq.*

2   From John Kessler's 'Sabbata' (1540)

The *Sabbata* of John Kessler (1503-74) are among the most fascinating of historical chronicles. He wrote them during holidays for his small sons, and they abound in vivid little stories. He had a journalist's flair for a scoop, and the most memorable of all his stories is of his encounter with Luther, still bearded and disguised ('Junker Georg') on his way back to Wittenberg. Naively and delightfully he entitles the episode:

HOW MARTIN LUTHER MET ME ON THE ROAD TO WITTENBERG

And here I cannot omit, though it may sound trivial and even childish to tell how Martin, on his way from his confinement back to Wittenberg, met me and my companion. As we made our way to Wittenberg, for the sake of studying holy scripture we came to Jena in the land of Thuringia (and God knows, in awful weather!) and after much enquiry in the town, for an inn where we might pass the night, we could find none and were turned away again and again, for it was Shrove Tuesday and nobody had time for strangers or pilgrims.

So we thought we would go out of town, and try the villages, and see if one of those would put us up for the night. At the town gate we met a respectable man who addressed us and asked us whither we were going at such a late hour, for there was neither house nor hearth in the whole neighbourhood, and as we stood a good chance of getting lost, he advised us to stay where we were. We answered, 'Good sir, we have tried all the inns, but everywhere we have been refused lodging.' Then he said, 'Did you try the Black Bear?' We said, 'No, where is it?' – so he showed us this inn just outside the town. The landlord came to the door and whereas all the others had refused us, he took us in. He led us into the parlour. Here we found one man, all by himself at a table with a book propped in front of him. He greeted us kindly and beckoned us to sit at his table. But our shoes were so muddy, so full of dust and filth that we could not be at our ease in the parlour and sat down modestly on a bench by the door. Then he drank our health, which we could not refuse, and so reassured by his friendliness and neighbourliness we sat down at the table to which he had bidden us and ordered some wine, that we might return his toast.

We took him for a knight, as he sat there, dressed after the fashion of that country, with a red hood, plain doublet and hose, a sword at his side, his right hand on its hilt, the other on his book. Then he asked where we came from, and gave the answer himself: 'You are Swiss. From whereabouts in Switzerland?' We answered, 'From St. Gallen.' Whereupon he said, 'If, as I imagine, you are going to Wittenberg, you will find two good compatriots there, Dr Jerome Schürpf and his brother, Dr Augustine.' We said, 'We have letters of introduction to them,' and then we asked, 'Sir, can you tell us whether Dr Martin Luther is in Wittenberg just now, or where else he may be?' He replied, 'I know for certain that he is not in Wittenberg at this moment. But Philip Melanchthon is there and he teaches Greek and others teach Hebrew.' And he advised us strongly to study these two languages which were above all needful for the study of holy scripture. We cried, 'God be praised, for we will not give up until we see and hear this man, if God spares us. For we have made this journey on his account, for we have heard that he would overthrow priestcraft and the Mass, which he says is an unscriptural form of worship, while we have been destined by our parents from youth, to be priests.' After this exchange he asked, 'And where have you been studying until now?' I answered, 'At Basle.' He asked, 'And how are things in Basle? Is Erasmus there? What is he doing?' 'As far as we know, he is all right. What he is doing nobody knows for he keeps quiet and stays at home.' And so we marvelled at this knight who knew all about the two Schürpfs and about Philip and Erasmus, and about how useful it was to know Greek and Hebrew: he also let slip an occasional Latin word so that we thought this must be a very uncommon knight.

'My boys,' he asked, 'what do they think about this Luther in Switzerland?' 'Sir, there are many different opinions. Some cannot extol him too highly and thank God for revealing truth and confounding error through him, but others revile him as an unconscionable heretic, especially the clergy.' He said, 'That I understand – those parsons!' This conversation having broken the ice, my companion took the book from his hand and opened it – and found it was a Hebrew Psalter. He put it down on the table again and the knight picked it up. At this we wondered still more, who he might be. My comrade cried, 'I'd have my little finger cut off if I might only learn this language.' To which the stranger answered, 'You can soon master it, if you stick to it, as I am doing. I do a bit each day.'

As the day was spent and darkness fell, the landlord came to set the table. Because he knew of our wish to see Martin Luther he said, 'Fellows, you would have had your wish if you had been here two days ago. He sat at this very table – he pointed with his finger – in that very place.' This was a big disappointment to us and we vented our rage on the bad state of the road which had led us to miss him. 'Still,' we said, 'at least we are in the house and at the table where he sat'. At this the landlord hid a smile and went out of the door and after a little beckoned me to him and said, 'Because you have such a sincere desire to see Martin Luther – there he is sitting next to you.' I thought he was having me on, and said, 'You're joking because you know how much I long to see him.' He said, 'It's the truth, but don't let on that you know who he is.' So I went back into the parlour and would fain share my news with my companion. I leaned over to him and whispered, 'The landlord just told me – don't look now, but that man is Martin Luther.' But he too was loath to believe it and said, 'No, you must have misheard. It must be Ulrich von Hutten' (for certainly the knight's dress and bearing were more like Hutten than Luther, the monk). I thought he must be right, for the beginning of each name ('Hut' – and 'Lut') sound similar, so I now behaved as though I were in the presence of Ulrich von Hutten.

Then two commercial travellers came in who also wanted lodging for the night. After they had taken off their cloaks and dried them, one of them put an unbound book at his side. Then Martin asked what book that was. He answered, 'It is Dr Luther's exposition of certain Gospels and Epistles, just printed and newly published. Haven't you seen it?' Martin answered, 'I shall get a copy soon.' Then the landlord said, 'Come to the table. Dinner is served!' We asked him to be patient with us and give us something separately. He said, 'My dear boys, sit up to table, I won't overcharge you.' But when Martin heard this he said. 'Come up here. I'll look after the bill.'

During that dinner Martin kept up edifying and friendly conversation, so that both the commercial travellers and we ourselves thought more about his words than about the food. Among other things he complained with sighing how at this time the German princes and nobles were assembled in Diet in Nuremberg, on account of God's Word, and the ups and downs and grievances of the affairs of the German nation, but were only concerned to have a good time, with costly tournaments, sleigh rides, vanities and whoring, instead of coming before God with fear and earnest prayer. 'But there's your Christian princes for you!' He further said that he hoped that the Gospel truth might have more fruit among our children and the next generation, than among the parents, since these were not poisoned with Popish error, but taught in plain truth based on the Word of God. With the parents, error was so deep rooted that it could not easily be plucked out.

Then the two merchants spoke their mind and the older one said, 'I am a plain, simple layman, and I don't understand much about this business. But this I do say. Either this Luther is an angel from heaven, or he is a devil from hell. I wouldn't mind giving ten guilders if I might make my confession to him, for I think he knows about quietening consciences.' Meanwhile the landlord came up and said, 'Don't worry about the bill. Martin paid for you.' And this really thrilled us, not the money or the food, but to have been the guest of such a man. After dinner, the travellers went to the stable to see about their horses. Martin remained alone with us in the parlour. Then we thanked him for his hospitality, saying that we took him to be Ulrich von Hutten. He said, 'No, I am not.' At this the landlord came in and Martin said, 'I've become a nobleman this evening. These Swiss think I am Ulrich von Hutten.' The landlord said, 'Not you. You're Martin Luther'. Then he laughed and said in jest – 'They take me for Hutten. You say I am Luther. Soon I shall be Marcolf.' Then he took a tall glass of beer and said in the manner of that country, 'Now you two Swiss, let us drink together a friendly drink, for our evening Grace.' But as I went to take the glass from him, he changed his mind and said, 'You aren't used to our outlandish beer; come, drink wine instead.' Then he stood up and threw his soldier's cloak over his shoulder. He gave us his hand and said, 'When you get to Wittenberg, give my greeting to Dr Schürpf.' We said, 'Willingly, but what is your name, that we may tell him who greets him?' Then he said, 'Just say, "He that should come sends his greeting." He'll understand.' Then he took his leave and went to bed.

Afterwards the commercial travellers came back into the parlour and

D

ordered more wine and talked for a long time about the identity of the guest. Then the landlord dropped the hint that he was Martin Luther, and when they took it in they were grieved and worried that they had spoken so casually in front of him, and made up their minds to get up early before he left and beg his pardon and not to take their words amiss, as they had not realized who he was.

So it was, for next morning they met him in the stable. But Martin answered them, 'You said at supper last night you would give ten guilders if you could only make confession to Luther. If you have really confessed, you must see and know whether I am Martin Luther.' He did not stay for further acquaintance but swung into his saddle and made off for Wittenberg.

On Saturday, then, (Luther had gone off on Friday) before the first Sunday in Lent we waited on Dr Jerome Schürpf in order to present our letters to him. When we were called into the parlour, behold – Martin Luther in the same get-up, as in Jena, and with him, Philip Melanchthon, Justus Jodocus Jonas, Nicholas Amsdorf, in addition to Dr Augustine Schürpf. Martin was telling them about what had happened to him during his absence from Wittenberg. Then he greeted us and laughed and pointing with his finger said, 'This is Philip Melanchthon I was telling you about.' Then Philip turned to us and asked us all kinds of questions about what had happened and we answered him as best we could. So we spent a whole day with these men, with great joy and a burning desire to know them better.

German in John Kessler, *Sabbata*, edited by Emil Egli. St. Gallen, 1902, 76 *et seq.*★

3   To Spalatin, 30 March 1522

All hail! I send you the letter you were expecting, my Spalatin. I cannot remember what I wrote to Duke John Frederick, except that I advised him not to introduce innovations unless it could be done without giving offence to the weak, and that all must be done in love. I wrote the same to Duke Karl.

I have not only translated the Gospel of St. John in my Patmos, but the whole of the New Testament, and Philip and I are now busy correcting it, and, with God's help, it will be a splendid work. Meantime we need your help, to find out proper words: therefore be ready to supply us with the common terms for some things we require, but not those used at court, for this book is to be written in the simplest language that all may understand it; and so that I may begin at once, send the names of the precious stones mentioned in *Revelation* XXI, and would that you could get permission from court to let us have the loan of some to see what they are like. . . .

WITTENBERG   MARTIN LUTHER
                                                   Currie, 102 *et seq.*

4 To Spalatin, 4 July 1522

Grace and peace in Christ! I hope, dear Spalatin, that you have received the Gospel of St. Mark and the Epistle to the Romans, with letters from good friends. The Gospel of St. Luke and the two Epistles to the Corinthians will soon be finished. I must reply to the growling lion who calls himself King of England. The ignorance the book displays is not to be wondered at in a royal author, but the bitterness and lies are gigantic. How Satan rages! But I shall embitter him more. . . .

WITTENBERG   MARTIN LUTHER
                                                   Currie, 107

5 On Translating: An Open Letter, 1530

. . . I have received your letter . . . to which you ask my reply. Why in translating the words of Paul, in the third chapter of Romans, *Arbitramur, hominem justificari ex fide absque operibus*, did I render them thus: 'We hold that man is justified without the works of the law, only by faith'? You tell me that the papists are making a tremendous fuss, because the word *sola*, 'only' is not in Paul's text, and this addition of my own to God's Word is not to be tolerated. . . .

. . . I translated the New Testament to the best of my ability and according to my conscience. . . . No one is forbidden to do a better piece of work. . . . It is my Testament and my translation, and it shall continue to be mine. If I have made some mistakes in it – though I am not conscious of any and would be most unwilling to give a single letter a wrong translation intentionally – I will not suffer the Papists to be the judges. . . . I know very well, and they know even less than the miller's beast, how much knowledge, work, reason and understanding is required in a good translator; they have never tried it. . . .

Please give these asses no other and no further answer to their blathering about the word *sola* than simply this: 'Luther will have it so, and he is a doctor above all the doctors of the whole Papacy.' . . .

To you and to our people, however, I shall show why I chose to use the word *sola*. . . . I have constantly tried, in translating, to produce a pure and clear German, and it has often happened that for two or three or four weeks we have sought and asked for a single word, and sometimes have not found it even then. In working at the book of Job, Master Philip, Aurogallus, and I could sometimes scarcely finish three lines in four days. Now that it is translated and complete, anyone can read and criticize it, and one now runs his eyes over three or four pages and does not stumble once. But he is not aware of the humps and lumps out of the way so that one could slide over it so finely. It is good ploughing when the field is cleaned up; but rooting out the woods and the stumps and getting the field ready, – that is work that nobody wants. . . .

Here, in *Romans* III, I know right well that the word *solum* was not in the Greek or Latin text and had no need of the Papists to teach me that. It is a fact that these four letters *s-o-l-a* are not there, and at these letters the asses-heads stare, like a cow at a new door. At the same time they do not see that the sense of them is there and that the word belongs there if the translation is to be clear and strong. I wanted to speak German, not Latin or Greek. . . . But it is the nature of our German language that in speaking of two things, one of which is admitted and the other denied, we use the word 'only' along with the word 'not' or 'no'. So we say, 'The farmer brings only grain and no money'; 'No, I have no money now, but only grain'; 'I have only eaten and not drunk'; 'Did you only write it, and not read it over?' There are innumerable cases of this kind in daily use.

In all these phrases it is the German usage, even though it is not the Latin or Greek usage, and it is the way of the German language to add the word 'only', in order that the word 'not' or 'no' may be more complete and clearer. . . .

We must not, like these asses, ask the Latin letters how we are to speak German; but we must ask the mother in the home, the children on the street, the common man in the marketplace about this, and look them in the mouth to see how they speak, and afterwards do our translating. . . .

For example, Christ says, *Ex abundantia cordis os loquitur*. If I am to follow the asses, they will lay the letters before me and translate thus: 'Out of the surplus of the heart, the mouth speaketh.' Tell me, is that German? . . . The mother in the home and the common man say,

'What fills the heart overflows the mouth.' That is speaking good German, the kind that I have tried for and, unfortunately, have not always reached or hit upon; for the Latin letters are a great hindrance to good German speech. . . .

This I can testify with a good conscience, – I have been faithful and diligent to the utmost in this work and have never had any purpose to falsify. I have not taken a single heller for it, or sought one, or made one by it. Nor have I had any intention to win honour by it – that God, my Lord, knows. . . .

I have not disregarded literal meanings too freely, but with my helpers, I have been very careful to see that when a passage is important, I have kept the literal meaning, and not departed freely from it. For example, in *John* VI, Christ says, 'Him hath God the Father sealed'. It would have been better German to say, 'On him hath God the Father put his mark,' or 'It is he whom God the Father means.' But I preferred to do violence to the German language, rather than depart from the words. Translating is not an art that everyone can practise, as the mad saints think; it requires a right pious, faithful, diligent, God-fearing, experienced, practised heart. . . .

However, I was not only relying on the nature of the languages and following that when, in *Romans* III, I inserted the word *solum*, 'only', but the text itself and the sense of St Paul demanded it and forced it upon me. He is dealing, in that passage, with the main point of Christian doctrine, that is, that we are justified by faith in Christ, without any works of the law, and he cuts away all works so completely, as even to say that the works of the law, though it is God's law and his Word, do not help us to righteousness. He cites Abraham as an example and says that he was justified so entirely without works, that even the highest work, which had then been newly commanded by God, before and above all other works, namely circumcision, did not help him to righteousness, but he was justified by faith, without circumcision and without any works at all. So he says, in chapter IV, 'If Abraham was justified by works, he may glory, but not before God.' But when works are so completely cut away, the meaning of it must be that faith alone justifies, and one who would speak plainly and clearly about this cutting away of all works, must say, 'Faith alone justifies us, and not works.' The matter itself, and not the nature of the language only, compels this translation.

'Nay,' say they, 'it has an offensive sound, and the common people understand it to mean that they need do no good works.' Dear sir, what are we to say? Is it not much more offensive that St. Paul himself does not say 'faith alone', but makes it even plainer and goes to the very limit, and says 'without the works of the law'? In *Galatians* I, also, and in many other places, he says 'Not by the works of the law.' A gloss might be found for the words 'faith alone,' but the words 'without the works of the law' are so plain and offensive and scandalous that they cannot be helped out by any gloss. How much rather might people learn not to do any good works, when they hear this preaching about works put in such plain, strong words: 'No works', 'without works', 'not by works'! If it is not offensive when one preaches 'without works', 'no works', 'not by works', why should it be offensive when one preaches, 'by faith alone'?

And what is still more of an offence, St. Paul does not reject simple, common works, but 'the works of the law'. From that it would be quite possible for someone to take offence and say that the law is condemned and accursed before God, and we ought to do nothing but evil, as the people said, in *Romans* III, 'Let us do evil that good may come'. . . . Dear man, St. Paul and we wanted to give this offence, and we preach so strongly against works and insist on faith alone, for no other reason than that people may be offended and stumble and fall, in order that they may learn to know that they do not become righteous by good works, but only by Christ's death and resurrection. Now if they cannot become righteous by the good works of the law, how much less shall they become righteous by bad works, and without the law! It does not follow, therefore, that because good works do not help, bad works do help; any more than it follows that because the sun cannot help a blind man to see, night and darkness must, therefore, help him to see.

I am surprised that anyone can make such a fuss over a matter as evident as this. Tell me whether Christ's death and resurrection are works of ours that we are to do, or not. They are not our works or the works of any law. Now it is only Christ's death and resurrection that make us free from sin, and righteous, as Paul says in *Romans* IV, 'He died for our sins and rose for our justification.' Tell me, further, what is the work by which we seize and hold Christ's death and resurrection? It cannot be any external work, but only the eternal faith that is in the heart. Faith alone, nay, all alone, without any works, seizes this death and resurrection when it is preached by the Gospel. . . .

I am not the only one of the first to say that faith alone justifies. Ambrose said it before me, and Augustine and many others; and if a man is going to read St. Paul and understand him, he will have to say the same thing and can say nothing else. . . .

The matter itself demands, then, that it be said, 'Faith alone justifies',

and the nature of our German language teaches us to express it that way·
I have the precedent of the holy Fathers also, and the peril of the people
compels me to it, so that they may not continue to hang upon works
and be without faith, and lose Christ, especially in these days, when they
have been so long accustomed to works and have to be torn away from
them by force. Therefore, it is not only right but highly necessary to
speak out as plainly and fully as possible, and say, 'Faith alone, without
works, justifies'. I am only sorry that I did not also add the words *alle*
and *aller*, and say, 'without any works of any laws', so that it would
have been said fully and roundly. Therefore it shall stay in my New
Testament and, though all the Papal asses become mad and foolish, they
shall not get it out. . . .   *Philad. Edn.*, V, 10 *et seq.*

6   Introduction to the Old Testament 1545 (1523)

Extracts from Luther's Biblical Introduction and Prefaces are grouped together
here for convenience, in spite of their separate dates of composition.

There are some who have a small opinion of the Old Testament, thinking of it as a book that was given to the Jewish people only, and is now
out of date, containing only stories of past times. They think that they
have enough in the New Testament and pretend to seek in the Old
Testament only a spiritual sense. Origen, Jerome and many persons of
high standing have held this view, but Christ says, 'Search in the scriptures, for they give testimony of me', and St. Paul bids Timothy continue in the reading of the scriptures, and declares, in *Romans* I, that
the Gospel was promised by God in the scriptures, and in *I Corinthians*
xv, he says that Christ came of the seed of David, died, and rose from
the dead, according to the scriptures; and St. Peter, too, points us back,
more than once, to the scriptures.

   They do this in order to teach us that the scriptures of the Old Testament are not to be despised, but to be read, because they themselves
base the New Testament upon them, and prove it by them, and appeal
to them, as St. Luke writes, in *Acts* XVII, saying that they at Thessalonica
searched the scriptures daily to discover whether it agreed with what
Paul taught. The ground and proof of the New Testament are surely
not to be despised, and therefore the Old Testament is to be highly
regarded. And what is the New Testament except an open preaching
and proclamation of Christ, appointed by the saying of the Old Testament and fulfilled by Christ? . . .

I beg and faithfully warn every pious Christian not to stumble at the simplicity of the language and the stories that will often meet him there. He should not doubt that however simple they may seem, these are the very words, works, judgements, and deeds of the high majesty, power, and wisdom of God; for this is scripture, and it makes fools of all the wise and prudent, and stands open to the small and foolish, as Christ says, in *Matthew* XI. Therefore let your own thoughts and feelings go, and think of the scriptures as the loftiest and noblest of holy things, as the richest of mines, which can never be worked out, so that you may find the wisdom of God that he lays before you in such foolish and simple guise, in order that he may quench all pride. Here you will find the swaddling-clothes and the mangers in which Christ lies, and to which the angel points the shepherds. Simple and little are the swaddling-clothes, but dear is the treasure, Christ, that lies in them.

Know, then, that the Old Testament is a book of laws, which teaches what men are to do and not to do, and gives, besides, examples and stories of how these laws are kept or broken; just as the New Testament is a Gospel-book, or book of grace, and teaches where one is to get the power to fulfill the law. But in the New Testament there are given, along with the teaching about grace, many other teachings that are laws and commandments for the ruling of the flesh, since in this life the spirit is not perfected and grace alone cannot rule. Just so in the Old Testament there are, beside the laws, certain promises and offers of grace, by which the holy fathers and prophets, under the law, were kept, like us, under the faith of Christ. Nevertheless, just as the peculiar and chief teaching of the New Testament is the proclamation of grace and peace in Christ, through the forgiveness of sins; so the peculiar and chief teaching of the Old Testament is the teaching of laws, the showing of sin, and the furtherance of good. Know that this is what you have to expect in the Old Testament. . . .   *Philad. Edn.*, VI, 367 *et seq.*

7   Preface to the Psalter, 1531

Many of the holy fathers praised and loved the Psalter above all other books of scripture; and although the work itself gives praise enough to its master, nevertheless we must give evidence of our own praise and thanks. . . .

I hold that no book of examples or legends of the saints finer than the Psalter has ever come, or can come, to the earth. . . . For here we find not only what one or two saints have done, but what He has done who is the head of all saints, and what the saints still do – the attitude they take towards God, towards friends and enemies, the way they conduct themselves in all dangers and sufferings. . . .

The Psalter ought to be a dear and beloved book, if only because it promises Christ's death and resurrection so clearly, and so typifies his kingdom and the condition and nature of all Christendom that it might well be called a little Bible. It puts everything that is in all the Bible most beautifully and briefly, and is made an *Enchiridion*, or hand-book, so that I have a notion that the Holy Ghost wanted to take the trouble to compile a short Bible and example-book of all Christendom, or of all saints. Thus, whoever could not read the whole Bible would here have almost an entire summary of it, comprised in one little book.

But above all this, the Psalter has this fine virtue and quality: other books make great ado over the works of the saints, but say very little about their words; but the Psalter is a pattern; it gives forth so sweet a fragrance, when one reads it, because it tells not only the works of the saints, but also their words, how they spoke with God and prayed, and still speak and pray. The other legends and examples, when compared to the Psalter, present to us only dumb saints; but the Psalter pictures really bold, living saints. . . .

In a word, would you see the holy Christian Church painted in living colour and form and put in one little picture? Then take up the Psalter and you have a fine, bright, pure mirror that will show you what the Church is; nay, you will find yourself also in it and the true *know thyself*, and God himself, besides, and all creatures.

Philad. Edn., 384 *et seq.*

8 Preface to the New Testament, 1545 (1522)

. . . Just as the Old Testament is a book in which are written God's laws and commandments, together with the history of those who kept and of those who did not keep them; so the New Testament is a book in which are written the Gospel and the promises of God, together with the history of those who believe and of those who do not believe them. For Gospel is a Greek word, and means in Greek, a good message, good tidings, good news, a good report, which one sings and tells with rejoicing. So, when David overcame the great Goliath, there came among the Jewish people the good report and encouraging news that their terrible enemy had been smitten and they had been rescued and given joy and peace; and they sang and danced and were glad for it.

So the Gospel, too, is a good story and report, sounded forth into all the world by the apostles, telling of a true David who strove with sin, death and devil, and overcame them, and thereby rescued all those who were captive in sin, afflicted with death, and overpowered by the devil. He made them righteous, gave them life, and saved them, so that they were given peace and brought back to God. For this they sing, and thank and praise God, and are glad forever, if only they believe firmly and are steadfast in faith.

This report and encouraging tidings, or evangelical and divine news, is also called a New Testament, because it is a testament, when a dying man bequeaths his property, after his death, to heirs whom he names, and Christ, before his death commanded and bequeathed this Gospel to be preached into all the world, and thereby gave to all who believe, as their possession, everything that he had, that is, his life, in which he swallowed up death; his righteousness, by which he blotted out sin; his salvation, with which he overcame everlasting damnation. A poor man, dead in sin and tied for hell, can hear nothing more comforting than this precious and tender message about Christ, and from the bottom of his heart, he must laugh and be glad over it, if he believes it true. . . .

John's Gospel and St. Paul's Epistles, especially that to the Romans, and St. Peter's first Epistle are the true kernel and marrow of all the books. . . .

In them you find not many works and miracles of Christ described, but you do find it depicted, in masterly fashion, how faith in Christ overcomes sin, death and hell, and gives life, righteousness and salvation. This is the real nature of the Gospel, and you have heard.

If I had to do without one or the other – either the works or preaching of Christ – I would rather do without his works than his preaching; for the works do not help me, but his words give life, as he himself says. Now John writes very little about the works of Christ, but very much about his preaching, while the other Evangelists write much of his works and little of his preaching; therefore John's Gospel is the one, tender, true chief Gospel, far, far to be preferred to the other three and placed high above them. So, too, the Epistles of St. Paul and St. Peter far surpass the other three Gospels – Matthew, Mark and Luke.

In a word, St. John's Gospel and his first Epistle, St. Paul's Epistles, especially *Romans*, *Galatians* and *Ephesians*, and St. Peter's first Epistle are the books that show you Christ and teach you all that it is necessary and good for you to know, even though you were never to see or hear any other book or doctrine. Therefore St. James' Epistle is really an epistle of straw, compared to them; for it has nothing of the nature of the Gospel about it. . . .
                                                                 Philad. Edn., 439 *et seq.*

9   Preface to the Epistle to the Romans, 1522[1]

This Epistle is really the chief part of the New Testament and the very purest Gospel, and is worthy not only that every Christian should know it word for word, by heart, but occupy himself with it every day, as the daily bread of the soul. It can never be read or pondered too much, and the more it is dealt with the more precious it becomes, and the better it tastes. . . .

It is, in itself, a bright light, almost enough to illume all the scripture.

To begin with we must have knowledge of its language and know what St. Paul means by the words, law, sin, grace, faith, righteous, flesh, spirit, etc., otherwise no reading of it has any value. . . .

Faith is not that human notion and dream that some hold for faith. Because they see that no betterment of life and no good works follow it, and yet they can hear and say much about faith, they fall into error, and say, 'Faith is not enough; one must do works in order to be righteous and be saved.' This is the reason that, when they hear the Gospel, they fall to – and make for themselves, by their own powers, an idea in their hearts, which says, 'I believe.' This they hold for true faith. But it is a human imagination and idea that never reaches the depths of the heart, and so nothing comes of it and no betterment follows it.

Faith, however, is a divine work in us. It changes us and makes us to be born anew of God (*John* 1); it kills the old Adam and makes altogether different men, in heart and spirit and mind and powers, and it brings with it the Holy Ghost. O, it is a living, busy, active, mighty thing, this faith; and so it is impossible for it not to do good works incessantly. It does not ask whether there are good works to do, but before the question rises it has already done them, and is always at the doing of them. He who does not these works is a faithless man. He gropes and looks about after faith and good works, and knows neither what faith is nor what good works are, though he talks and talks, with many words, about faith and good works.

Faith is a living, daring confidence in God's grace, so sure and certain that a man would stake his life on it a thousand times. This confidence in God's grace and knowledge of it makes men glad and bold and happy in dealing with God and with all his creatures; and this is the work of the Holy Ghost in faith. Hence a man is ready and glad, without compulsion, to do good to everyone, to serve everyone, to suffer everything,

---

[1] For a beautiful version of this in sixteenth-century English by William Tyndale see *The New Testament, translated by William Tyndale, 1534*, edited by N. H. Wallis, Cambridge University Press, 1938.

in love and praise of God, who has shown him this grace; and thus it is impossible to separate works from faith, quite as impossible as to separate heat and light from fire. . . .

Righteousness, then, is such a faith and is called 'God's righteousness', or 'the righteousness that avails before God', because God gives it and counts it as righteousness for the sake of Christ, our mediator, and makes a man give to every man what he owes him. For through faith a man becomes sinless and comes to take pleasure in God's commandments; thus he gives to God the honour that is his and pays him what he owes him; but he also serves man willingly, by whatever he can, and thus pays his debt to everyone. Such righteousness nature and free will and all our powers cannot bring into existence. No one can give himself faith; and no more can he take away his own unbelief; how, then, will he take away a single sin, even the very smallest? Therefore, all that is done, apart from faith, or in unbelief, is false; it is hypocrisy and sin, no matter how good a show it makes (*Romans* xiv).

You must not so understand flesh and spirit as to think that flesh has to do only with unchastity and spirit only with what is inward, in the heart; but Paul, like Christ, in *John* iii, calls 'flesh' everything that is born of the flesh; that is, the whole man, with body and soul, mind and senses, because everything about him longs for the flesh. Thus you should learn to call him 'fleshly' who thinks, teaches, and talks a great deal about high spiritual matters, but without grace. From the 'works of the flesh', in *Galatians* v, you can learn that Paul calls heresy and hatred 'works of the flesh', and in *Romans* viii, he says that 'the law was weak through the flesh', and this does not refer to unchastity, but to all sins, above all to unbelief, which is the most spiritual of all vices. On the other hand, he calls him a spiritual man who is occupied with the most external kind of works, as Christ, when he washed the disciples' feet, and Peter, when he steered his boat, and fished. Thus 'the flesh' is a man who lives and works, inwardly and outwardly, in the service of the flesh's profit and of this temporal life; 'the spirit' is the man who lives and works, inwardly and outwardly, in the service of the Spirit and the future life. . . .

But do you follow the order of this Epistle? Worry first about Christ and the Gospel, that you may recognise your sin and his grace; then fight your sin, as the first eight chapters here have taught; then, when you have reached the eighth chapter, and are under the cross and suffering, that will teach you the right doctrine of predestination, in the ninth, tenth and eleventh chapters, and how comforting it is. For in the absence of suffering and the cross and the danger of death, one cannot deal with predestination without harm and without secret wrath against God. The old Adam must die before he can endure this subject and drink the strong wine of it. Therefore take heed not to drink wine while you are still a suckling. There is a limit, a time, an age for every doctrine. . . .

Thus in this Epistle we find most richly the things that a Christian ought to know; namely, what is law, Gospel, sin, punishment, grace, faith, righteousness, Christ, God, good works, love, hope, the cross, and also how we are to conduct ourselves towards everyone, whether righteous or sinner, strong or weak, friend or foe. All this is ably founded on scripture and proved by his own example and that of the prophets. Therefore it appears that St. Paul wanted to comprise briefly in this one Epistle the whole Christian and evangelical doctrine and to prepare an introduction to the entire Old Testament; for, without doubt, he who has this Epistle well in his heart, has the light and power of the Old Testament with him. Therefore let every Christian exercise himself in it habitually and continually. To this may God give His grace. Amen.

Philad. Edn., 447 *et seq.*

10   Preface to the Epistle of Saint James, 1545 (1522)

Though this Epistle of St. James was rejected by the ancients, I praise it and hold it a good book, because it sets up no doctrine of men and lays great stress upon God's law. But to state my own opinion about it, though without injury to anyone, I consider that it is not the writing of any apostle. My reasons are as follows.

First: flatly against St. Paul and all the rest of scripture, it ascribes righteousness to works and says that Abraham was justified by his works, in that he offered his son Isaac; though St. Paul on the contrary teaches, in *Romans* IV, that Abraham was justified without works, by faith alone, before he offered his son, and proves it by Moses in *Genesis* XV. Now although this Epistle might be helped and a gloss be found for this work-righteousness, it cannot be defended against applying to works the saying of Moses in *Genesis* XV, which speaks only of Abraham's faith, and not of his works, as St. Paul shows in *Romans* IV. This fault, therefore, leads to the conclusion that it is not the work of any Apostle.

Second: its purpose is to teach Christians, and in all this long teaching it does not once mention the Passion, the Resurrection, or the Spirit of Christ. He names Christ several times, but he teaches nothing about him, and only speaks of common faith in God. For it is the duty of a true Apostle to preach of the Passion and Resurrection and work of Christ, and thus lay the foundation of faith, as he himself says, in *John* xv, 'Ye shall bear witness of me.' All the genuine sacred books agree in this, that all of them preach Christ and deal with him. That is the true test, by which to judge all books, when we see whether they deal with Christ or not, since all the scriptures show us Christ (*Romans* III) and St. Paul will know nothing but Christ (*I Corinthians* xv). What does not teach Christ is not Apostolic, even though St. Peter or Paul taught it; again, what preaches Christ would be Apostolic, even though Judas, Annas, Pilate and Herod did it.

But this James does nothing more than drive to the law and its works; and he mixes the two up in such disorderly fashion that it seems to me he must have been some good, pious man, who took some sayings of the Apostles' disciples and threw them thus on paper; or perhaps they were written down by someone else from his preaching. He calls the law a 'law of liberty', though St. Paul calls it a law of slavery, of wrath, of death and of sin (*Galatians* III; *Romans* VII).

Moreover, in chapter v, he quotes the sayings of St. Peter, 'Love covereth the multitude of sins' (*I Peter* IV) and 'Humble yourselves under the hand of God' (*I Peter*), and of St. Paul (*Galatians* v), 'The Spirit lusteth against hatred'; and yet, in point of time, St. James was put to death by Herod, in Jerusalem, before St. Peter. So it seems that he came long after St. Peter and St. Paul.

In a word, he wants to guard against those who relied on faith without works, and is unequal to the task . . . and would accomplish by insisting on the Law what the Apostles accomplish by inciting men to love. Therefore, I cannot put him among the chief books, though I would not thereby prevent anyone from putting him where he pleases and estimating him as he pleases; for there are many good sayings in him.

Philad. Edn., 477 *et seq.*

11   Preface to the Revelation of Saint John, 1522

About this book of the Revelation of John, I leave everyone free to hold his own ideas, and would bind no man to my opinion or judgement; I say what I feel. I miss more than one thing in this book, and this makes me hold it to be neither Apostolic nor prophetic. . . .

Philad. Edn., 488 *et seq.*

12 Preface to the Revelation of Saint John, 1545

We can profit by this book and make good use of it. First, for our comfort! We can know that neither force nor lies, neither wisdom nor holiness, neither tribulation nor suffering shall suppress the Church, but it will gain the victory and overcome at last.

This article, 'I believe one holy, Christian Church', is an article of faith, as well as the rest. The reason, therefore, cannot recognize it, though it puts all its glasses on. The devil can cover it over with offences and tumults, so that you have to take offence at it. God, too, can hide it with faults and short-comings of all kinds, so that you become a fool and pass such judgement on it. It will not be known by sight, but by faith, and faith concerns the things we do not see (*Hebrews* xi); and the Church joins with her Lord in the song, 'Blessed is he that takes no offence in me.' A Christian, too, is hidden from himself; he does not see his holiness and virtue, but sees in himself only lack of virtue and of holiness; and you, dull wise man, would behold the Church with your blind reason and your unclean eyes!

In a word, our holiness is in heaven, and not in the world, before men's eyes, like goods in the market. Therefore, let there be offences and tumults and heresy and faults, and let them do what they can! If only the word of the Gospel remains pure among us, and we love and cherish it, we are not to doubt that Christ is with us, even when things are at their worst; for we see, in this book, that, through and above all plagues and beasts and bad angels, Christ is with his saints, and wins the victory at last.

Philad. Edn., 486 *et seq.*

N   THE WITTENBERG SERMONS, 1522

Luther's eight sermons, which he preached at Wittenberg immediately upon his return from the Wartburg, beginning Invocavit Sunday, 9 March 1522, were not only immediately effective in restoring order in Wittenberg, but put lucidly the difference in timing and method between Luther's reformation movement and the legalistic puritanism of Karlstadt and his radical friends.

1   Extracts from the Wittenberg Sermons, 1522

Here let us beware lest Wittenberg become Capernaum [*cf. Matthew* XI:23]. I notice that you have a great deal to say of the doctrine of faith and love which is preached to you, and this is no wonder; an ass can almost intone the lessons, and why should you not be able to repeat the doctrines and formulas? Dear friends, the kingdom of God – and we are that kingdom – does not consist in talk or words [*I Corinthians* IV:20], but in activity, in deeds, in works and exercises. God does not want hearers and repeaters of words [*James* 1:22], but followers and doers, and this occurs in faith through love. For a faith without love is not enough – rather it is not faith at all, but a counterfeit of faith, just as a face seen in a mirror is not a real face, but merely the reflection of a face [*I Corinthians* XIII:12]. . . .

I would not have gone so far as you have done, if I had been here. The cause is good, but there has been too much haste. For there are still brothers and sisters on the other side who belong to us and must still be won.

Let me illustrate. The sun has two properties, light and heat. No king has power enough to bend or guide the light of the sun; it remains fixed in its place. But the heat may be turned and guided, and yet is ever about the sun. Thus faith must always remain pure and immovable in our hearts, never wavering; but love bends and turns so that our neighbour may grasp it. There are some who can run, others must walk, still others can hardly creep [cf. I Corinthians VIII: 7-13]. Therefore we must not look upon our own, but upon our brother's powers, so that he who is weak in faith, and attempts to follow the strong, may not be destroyed of the devil. Therefore, dear brethren, follow me; I have never been a destroyer. And I was also the very first whom God called to this work. I cannot run away, but will remain as long as God allows. I was also the one to whom God first revealed that his Word should be preached to you. I am also sure that you have the pure Word of God. . . .

Dear friends, you heard yesterday the chief characteristics of a Christian man, that his whole life and being is faith and love. Faith is directed towards God, love toward man and one's neighbour, and consists in such love and service for him, as we have received from God without our work and merit. Thus, there are two things: the one, which is the most needful, and which must be done in one way and no other; the other, which is a matter of choice and not of necessity, which may be kept or not, without endangering faith or incurring hell. . . .

. . . to hold Mass in such a manner is sinful, and yet no one should be dragged away from it by the hair; for it should be left to God, and his Word should be allowed to work alone, without our work or interference. . . .

Now if I should rush in and abolish it by force, there are many who would be compelled to consent to it and yet not know where they stand, whether it is right or wrong, and they would say: I do not know if it is right or wrong, I do not know where I stand, I was compelled by force to submit to the majority. And this forcing and commanding results in a mere mockery, an external show, a fool's play, man-made ordinances, sham-saints, and hypocrites. For where the heart is not good I care nothing at all for the work. We must first win the hearts of the people. But that is done when I teach only the Word of God, preach the Gospel, and say: Dear lords or pastors, abandon the Mass, it is not right, you are sinning when you do it; I cannot refrain from telling you this. But I would not make it an ordinance for them, nor urge a general law. He who would follow me could do so, and he who refused would remain outside. In the latter case the Word would sink into the heart and do its work.

So when you have won the heart, you have won the man – and thus the thing must finally fall of its own weight and come to an end. And if the hearts and minds of all are agreed and united, abolish it. But if all are not heart and soul for its abolishment – leave it in God's hands, I beseech you, otherwise the result will not be good. Not that I would again set up the Mass; I let it lie in God's name. . . .

In short, I will preach it, teach it, write it, but I will constrain no man by force, for faith must come freely without compulsion. Take myself as an example. I opposed Indulgences and all the Papists, but never with force. I simply taught, preached, and wrote God's word; otherwise I did nothing. And while I slept [*cf. Mark* IV:26-9], or drank Wittenberg beer with my friends Philip [Melanchthon] and [Nicholas von] Amsdorf, the Word so greatly weakened the Papacy that no prince or emperor ever inflicted such losses upon it. I did nothing; the Word did everything. Had I desired to foment trouble, I could have brought great bloodshed upon Germany; indeed, I could have started such a game that even the emperor would not have been safe. But what would it have been? Mere fool's play. I did nothing; I let the Word do its work.

Now let us speak of the two kinds. Although I hold that it is necessary that the sacrament should be received in both kinds, according to the institution of the Lord, nevertheless it must not be made compulsory nor a general law. . . .

Amer. Edn., LI, 71 *et seq.*

2   Ordinance for a Common Chest at Leisnig, 1523

In scores of German and Swiss cities, besides Wittenberg, the civic authorities promulgated edicts reforming worship, and instituted machinery for administering secularized church property. The following ordinance is one of the best known.

In the name of the Holy and undivided Trinity. Amen.

We, the honourable men, council, aldermen, nobles, and commons of the town and parish of Leisnig, with its dependent villages. Whereas, through the grace of Almighty God and the revelation of the Christian evangelical scriptures, we have received not only a firm faith but a sure knowledge that all the inward and outward resources of believers should serve to the honour of God and the love of our neighbour, we give notice that, for ourselves and our posterity, we have resolved to maintain the following brotherly compacts in our community:

I. *Of Appointments to the Pastorate*
We will and shall always exercise our Christian freedom, so far as

concerns the appointment to our common pastorate and the call, election, admission, and dismissal of our common minister, for the sole preaching of God's word and dispensing of the sacraments, never otherwise than according to the disposition and order of divine scripture. . .

II. Of the Means, Provision, and Receipts of the Common Chest

In order that our Christian faith, in which all goods temporal and eternal are gotten and given us by the eternal God through our Lord and Saviour Jesus Christ, may bear its proper fruit in brotherly love. . . . we, the above-named common assembly of the parish, . . . have resolved to set up and maintain a common chest forthwith . . . in intention, manner, and form, as follows:

For the furnishing and provision of the common chest shall the following items, rents, goods, privileges, moneys, and possessions be everywhere collected together, to be and remain perpetually united.

(i) *Receipts from the goods and privileges of the benefice.* All the goods, privileges, fees-simple, quit-rents, rents, hereditaments, houses, yards, gardens, lands, meadows, stock, and chattels, without exception, belonging anywhere to the office of pastor and minister here among us . . . which we, the common assembly of the parish, in behalf of our common pastorate, have a reserved right to acquire, according to the tenor of the arrangement and decision therein between the abbey of Buch and us . . . , these as being available for our common chest, as also all that belongs to the school and the sacristy, we have paid into it.

(ii) *Receipts from the goods and privileges of the church.* All the goods, privileges, etc . . . , bridge-tolls, plate, jewels, etc. . . . belonging to our church shall, in their entirety, along with the written title-deeds, inventories, and registers concerning them, be gathered into and remain in the common chest.

(iii) *Receipts from the goods and privileges of the four altar endowments and other foundations.* The four altar-endowments in our church shall, as soon as the present chantry-priests die or the existing endowments are vacated, be no longer bestowed; but the four houses, together with the goods, rents, revenues, commodities, plate, etc., thereto belonging, shall be brought into the common chest; and further all celebrations, years' minds, Indulgence-weeks or octaves, and other several foundations and alms, for the hospital or elsewhere, shall all be paid into the common chest. . . .

V. Of Disbursements and Discharges from the Common Chest

Herein we, the parish assembly and our successors, will and shall provide for ourselves out of our common chest, through our ten elected managers (so far as our means with God's grace will permit), and arrange for disbursements, according to need, as follows:

(i)   *Disbursements for the pastorate.* Our common minister or pastor, together with our elected preacher appointed to assist him ... and chaplain besides, if need so require, shall be provided by the ten managers, according to the unanimous resolution of the whole assembly, with a specified sum of money, sundry means of support, and profits of lands and goods annually throughout the year, in quarterly instalments, payable at the quarter ... to be handed to them, in return for the proper receipt, out of the common chest. With such salaries, supplies, profits and maintenance they are to be content, and shall in no wise seek or receive anything further from their parishioners, unsought free-will offerings and gifts excepted. ...

Kidd, Doc. 64

3   On the Appointment of Ministers, November 1523

1. *DECLARATION*

In the first place I freely confess that if there are any who expect they are to receive from me, intact or improved, the rite and custom hitherto observed in shaving and anointing priests, then the contents of this little book will have no relevance for them. They are welcome to enjoy their own religion – or superstition, popularized as it is from ancient and widespread tradition. Our concern, however, is to seek the pure and genuine system [*rationem*] prescribed in holy scripture, and not to trouble ourselves with what custom or the Fathers have given us or done in this matter; once and for all we have learned that our duty is ... so far from obeying human traditions, openly to dominate them, as our purpose and our Christian liberty require. ...

2. *DISSUASION FROM ACCEPTING PAPAL ORDINATIONS*

... For the time being I will overlook the fact that in Papal ordinations these whom they call priests are anointed and appointed by the sole authority of the bishop; the consent or election of the people over whom they are to be placed is neither sought nor given. . . . Also, the majority are ordained only to what they call 'benefices'; their only duty will be to offer Masses. . . . As I say, however, I am willing to overlook this monstrous abuse in Papal ordinations for the time being.

Anyone who loves Christ must needs recoil from such a state of affairs, and endure any suffering rather than submit to Papal ordinations, since everything about them is transacted with the utmost . . . perversity. . . . For since ordination was instituted on the authority of scripture . . . in order to provide for the people ministers of the Word, it is (I maintain) this public ministry of the Word, by which are dispersed the mysteries of God, which ought to be instituted through holy ordination . . . , since without the Word nothing stands in the Church, and everything in it stands by the Word alone. But these Papists I am talking about do not even dream of a ministry like this in their ordinations. . . . Instead of ministers of the Word they ordain petty sacrificers, who offer masses and hear confessions. For this is what the bishop intends when he gives the chalice into their hand and confers the power of consecrating and sacrificing for the living and the dead. . . . In this way . . . he breathes the spirit into their ears and makes them confessors, saying 'Receive the Holy Spirit'. Such is this most resplendent power of consecration and absolution. . . .

But since it is quite certain that the mass is not a sacrifice, and that such confessions, which they would make obligatory, are nothing, both alike being the sacrilegious and lying inventions of men, it clearly follows that such sacred ordinations make nobody a priest or a minister in the sight of God [coram Deo]. . . . Therefore faith and conscience urge us, under penalty of the anathema of God, to beware of being ordained by them; indeed, the plan of our salvation enforces our abstention from their hateful and damnable ordinations.

3. *A PRIEST IS NOT THE SAME AS A PRESBYTER OR MINISTER: THE FORMER IS BORN, THE LATTER MADE*

And here the prime need is unswerving faith. . . . Hence, first of all, let it be to you as an immovable rock, that the New Testament knows nothing of any priest who is or can be anointed externally. If there are such, they are masks [larvae] and idols. . . . For a priest . . . is not made but born; not ordained but created. His birth indeed is not of the flesh but of the Spirit, by water and Spirit in the bath of regeneration [*John*

III:6, *Titus* III:5]. In a word, all Christians are priests and all priests Christians. . . .

But let us proceed, and show from what they call the priestly offices themselves that all Christians are equally priests. I have sufficiently treated elsewhere [*Address to the Christian Nobility*, W.A., VI, 407 *et seq.*] the words of *I Peter* II [:9] and *Revelation* V [:10]. The offices of a priest are, in the main, the following: to teach, to preach and proclaim the Word of God, to baptize, to consecrate or administer the Eucharist, to bind and loose sins, to pray for others, to sacrifice, to judge the doctrines and the spirits of all men. . . .

But all these things of which we have been speaking concern the common right of Christians: for since, as we have proved, all these things are common to all Christians, no man can step forward on his own authority and arrogate to himself what belongs to all. . . . But the rights of the community demand that one, or as many as the community decides, shall be chosen or accepted to perform these offices publicly in the place and the name of all, who have the same rights. Otherwise there would be shameful confusion among the people of God and another Babylon would arise in the Church. . . . For it is one thing to exercise a right in public, another to use it in emergency; and public exercise is only authorized by the consent of the whole community or the church, whereas in emergency whoever is willing may use it. . . .

All this, I believe, confirms the conclusion that those who preside over the sacraments or the Word among the people neither can nor ought to be called priests. The fact that they are called priests is a borrowing from heathen ritual or a relic of Jewish practice. . . . According to the Gospel writings, they would be better named ministers, deacons, Bishops, stewards (more frequently called presbyters on account of their age). As Paul says in *I Corinthians* IV: 'We must be regarded as ministers of Christ and stewards of the mysteries of God.' He does not say 'as priests of Christ', because he would know that the name and office of priest are the common possession of all. . . .

If ministers are as we say, then the 'indelible character' vanishes and the perpetuity of the priesthood is a mere fiction. A minister may be deposed if he ceases to be faithful, or reinstated as long as he deserves it or the community of the Church desires, just as any civil administrator among brethren of equal rights. . . .

By these . . . impregnable stays of scripture (if we believe the Word of God) that most dreadful need is overcome which hitherto has forced Bohemia to beg for a shaven priesthood and accept the most unworthy specimens it received. For here we have clearer than day . . . the source of priests or ministers of the Word: that is, from the very flock of Christ and no other source. For when clear proof has been given that everyone has the right of ministering the Word, and that he is even commanded to do so if he sees either a deficiency of teachers or wrongful teaching by those he has – as Paul lays down in *I Corinthians* XIV, to ensure the proclamation of the power of God among us all – how much more does a whole Christian community have the right and duty to commit this office by common vote to one or more in their stead? And these one or more in turn to others, if the common vote likewise approves? . . .

Necessity and the common mind of the faithful (*communis sensus fidei*) force the same conclusion. For since the Church is . . . nourished by the Word of God, it is patent that without the Word it cannot exist; if it loses the Word it ceases to be the Church. Hence if a man is born from his baptism for the ministry of the Word, and papal bishops are unwilling to bestow the ministry of the Word . . . the only thing left is either to let the Church of God perish without the Word or to allow the propriety of a church meeting to cast its votes and choose from its own resources one or as many as are necessary and suitable, and commend and confirm these to the whole community by prayer and the laying-on of hands. These should then be recognized and honoured as lawful bishops and ministers of the Word, in the assured faith that God himself is the author of what the common consent of the faithful has so performed – of those, that is, who accept and confess the Gospel. . . .

This, then, is what you should do. . . . Let those be called and come together freely whose heart God has so touched that they think and judge as you do yourselves: go forward in the name of the Lord to choose him or those whom you desire, and who are seen to be worthy and suitable. Then let those who have influence among you lay hands on them, and confirm and commend them . . . to the Church . . . and let them on this showing be your bishops, ministers, pastors. Amen. . . .

Latin in Kidd, *Documents*, 65*

4 Secular Authority: To what extent it should be obeyed

LETTER OF DEDICATION [to John, Duke of Saxony]

. . . Again, illustrious, high-born Prince, gracious Lord, necessity is laid upon me, and the entreaties of many and above all your Grace's wishes impel me, to write concerning the secular authorities and the sword they bear; how it should be used in a Christian manner and in how far men are bound to obey it. . . .

I hope, however, to instruct the princes and the secular authorities in such a way that they shall remain Christians and that Christ shall remain Lord, yet so that Christ's commandments need not for their sake be changed into counsels. . . .

Your Princely Grace's obedient servant, MARTIN LUTHER

WITTENBERG, *New Year's Day,* 1523

THE TREATISE

. . . We must divide all the children of Adam into two classes; the first, belong to the kingdom of God, the second to the kingdom of the world. Those belonging to the kingdom of God are all true believers in Christ and are subject to Christ. For Christ is the King and Lord in the kingdom of God, as the second Psalm and all the scriptures say. . . .

Now observe, these people need no secular sword or law. And if all the world were composed of real Christians, that is, true believers, no prince, king, lord, sword or law would be needed. For what were the use of them, since Christians have in their hearts the Holy Spirit, who instructs them and causes them to wrong no one, to love every one, willingly and cheerfully to suffer injustice and even death from every one. Where every wrong is suffered and every right is done, no quarrel, strife, trial, judge, penalty, law or sword is needed. Therefore, it is not possible for the secular sword and law to find any work to do among Christians, since of themselves they do much more than its laws and doctrines can demand. . . .

Why is this? Because the righteous does of himself all and more than all that all the laws demand. But the unrighteous do nothing that the law demands, therefore they need the law to instruct, constrain, and compel them to do what is good. A good tree does not need any teaching or law to bear good fruit, its nature causes it to bear according to its kind without any law and teaching. A man would be a fool to make a book of laws and statutes telling an apple tree how to bear apples and not thorns, when it is able by its own nature to do this better than man with all his books can define and direct. Just so, by the Spirit and by faith all Christians are throughout inclined to do well and keep the law, much more than any one can teach them with all the laws, and need so far as they are concerned no commandments nor law. . . .

All who are not Christians belong to the kingdom of the world and are under the law. Since few believe and still fewer live a Christian life, do not resist the evil, and themselves do no evil, God has provided for non-Christians a different government outside the Christian estate and God's kingdom, and has subjected them to the sword, so that, even though they would do so, they cannot practice their wickedness, and that, if they do, they may not do it without fear nor in peace and prosperity. . . .

If any one attempted to rule the world by the Gospel, and put aside all secular law and the secular sword, on the plea that all are baptized and Christian, and that according to the Gospel, there is to be among them neither law nor sword, nor necessity for either, pray, what would happen? He would loose the bands and chains of the wild and savage beasts, and let them tear and mangle every one, and at the same time say they were quite tame and gentle creatures; but I would have the proof in my wounds. . . .

It is indeed true that Christians, so far as they themselves are concerned, are subject to neither law nor sword and need neither; but first take heed and fill the world with real Christians before ruling it in a Christian and evangelical manner. This you will never accomplish; for the world and the masses are and always will be unchristian, although they are all baptized and are nominally Christian. Christians, however, are few and far between, as the saying is. Therefore it is out of the question that there should be a common Christian government over the whole world, nay even over one land or company of people, since the wicked always out-number the good. Hence a man who would venture to govern an entire country or the world with the Gospel would be like a shepherd who should place in one fold wolves, lions, eagles and sheep together and let them freely mingle with one another and say, Help yourselves, and be good and peaceful among yourselves; the fold is open, there is plenty of food; have no fear of dogs and clubs. The sheep, forsooth, would keep the peace and would allow themselves to be fed and governed in peace, but they would not live long; nor would any beast keep from molesting another.

For this reason these two kingdoms must be sharply distinguished, and both be permitted to remain; the one to produce piety, the other to bring about external peace and prevent evil deeds; neither is sufficient in the world without the other. For no one can become pious before God by means of the secular government, without Christ's spiritual rule. Hence Christ's rule does not extend over all, but Christians are always in the minority and are in the midst of non-Christians. . . .

Christians, among themselves and by and for themselves, need no law or sword, since it is neither necessary nor profitable for them. Since, however, a true Christian lives and labours on earth not for himself, but for his neighbour, therefore the whole spirit of his life impels him to do even that which he need not do, but which is profitable and necessary for his neighbour. Because the sword is a very great benefit and necessary to the whole world, to preserve peace, to punish sin and to prevent evil, he submits most willingly to the rule of the sword, pays tax, honours those in authority, serves, helps and does all he can to further the government, that it may be sustained and held in honour and fear. Although he needs none of these things for himself and it is not necessary for him to do them, yet he considers what is for the good and profit of others. . . .

You are under obligation to serve and further the sword by whatever means you can, with body, soul, honour or goods. For it is nothing that you need, but something quite useful and profitable for the whole world and for your neighbour. Therefore, should you see that there is a lack of hangmen, beadles, judges, lords or princes, and find that you are qualified, you should offer your services and seek the place, that necessary government may by no means be despised and become inefficient or perish. For the world cannot and dare not dispense with it. . . . Now, it should be quite unchristian to say that there is any service of God in which a Christian ought not and dare not take part, when such a service belongs to no one so much as to Christians. It would indeed be good and profitable if all princes were real and good Christians, for the sword and the government, as a special service of God, belong of right to Christians, more than to all other men on earth. Therefore you should cherish the sword or the government, even as the state of matrimony, or husbandry, or any other handiwork which God has instituted. . . .

But you ask further, whether the beadles, hangmen, jurists, advocates, and their ilk, can also be Christians and in a state of salvation. I answer: If the state and its sword are a divine service, as was proved above, that which the state needs in order to wield the sword must also be a divine service. There must be those who arrest, accuse, slay and destroy the wicked, and protect, acquit, defend and save the good. Therefore, when such duties are performed, not with the intention of seeking one's own ends, but only of helping to maintain the laws and the state, so that the wicked may be restrained, there is no peril in them and they may be followed like any other pursuit and be used as one's means of support. For, as was said, love of neighbour seeks not its own, considers not how great or how small, but how profitable and how needful for neighbour or community the works are. . . .

HOW FAR SECULAR AUTHORITY EXTENDS

. . . If then your prince or temporal lord commands you to hold with the Pope, to believe this or that, or commands you to give up certain books, you should say, It does not befit Lucifer to sit by the side of God. Dear lord, I owe you obedience with life and goods; command me within the limits of your power on earth, and I will obey. But if you command me to believe, and to put away books, I will not obey; for in this case you are a tyrant and overreach yourself, and command where you have neither right nor power, etc. Should he take your property for this, and punish such disobedience, blessed are you. Thank God that you are worthy to suffer for the sake of the divine Word, and let him rave, fool that he is. He will meet his judge. . . .

You must know that from the beginning of the world a wise prince is a rare bird indeed; still more so a pious prince. They are usually the greatest fools or the worst knaves on earth; therefore one must constantly expect the worst from them and look for little good from them, especially in divine matters, which concern the salvation of souls. They are God's jailers and hangmen, and his divine wrath needs them to punish the wicked and preserve outward peace. . . .

What, then, are the priests and bishops? I answer, their government is not one of authority or power, but a service and an office; for they are neither higher nor better than other Christians. Therefore they should not impose any law or decree on others without their will and consent; their rule consists in nothing else than in dealing with God's Word, leading Christians by it and overcoming heresy by its means. For, as was said, Christians can be ruled by nothing but by God's Word. . . .

[The Christian Prince or Lord] should picture Christ to himself, and say, 'Behold, Christ the chief ruler came and served me, sought not to have power, profit and honour from me, but only considered my need, and did all he could that I might have power, profit and honour from him and through him. I will do the same, not seek mine own advantage in my subjects, but their advantage, and thus serve them by my office, protect them, give them audience and support, that they, and not I, may have the benefit and profit by it.' Thus a prince should in his heart empty himself of his power and authority, and interest himself in the need of his subjects, dealing with it as though it were his own need. Thus

Christ did unto us; and these are the proper works of Christian love.

You say, Who then would be a prince? For that would make the position of a prince the worst on earth, full of trouble, labour and sorrow. Where would there be room for the princely pleasures, such as dancing, hunting, racing, gaming and similar worldly enjoyments? I answer, We are not prescribing now how a temporal prince shall be a Christian, in order that he also may reach heaven. Who does not know that a prince is a rare bird in heaven? . . .

But when a prince is in the wrong, are his people bound to follow him then too? I answer, No, for it is no one's duty to do wrong; we ought to obey God who desires the right, rather than men. How is it, when the subjects do not know whether the prince is in the right or not? I answer, As long as they cannot know, nor find out by any possible means, they may obey without peril to their souls. . . .

Therefore we will close by saying briefly that a prince's duty is fourfold: first, that towards God consists in true confidence and in sincere prayer; second, that towards his subjects consists in love and Christian service; third, that towards his counsellors and rulers consists in an open mind and unfettered judgement; fourth, that towards evil doers consists in proper zeal and firmness. Then his state is right, outwardly and inwardly, pleasing to God and to the people. But he must expect much envy and sorrow, – the cross will soon rest on the shoulders of such a ruler. . . .

Philad. Edn., III, 228 *et seq.*

5   To John Œcolampadius, 20 June 1524

Grace and peace in Christ! I beg you, dearest Œcolampadius, not to ascribe my not writing to you to ingratitude or sloth; for I have not heard from you since you quitted your order, and fancied that since Christ had strengthened your heart through the power of the Spirit, you had overcome your superstitious conscience, and were now too great to write me, or need a letter from me. Truly, I highly approve of the praiseworthy step you have taken, and Philip never ceases speaking of you, and rejoices that you keep him in remembrance.

May the Lord strengthen you in your great undertaking – the exposition of Isaiah – although I know Erasmus takes no pleasure therein. But do not let his displeasure disturb you. He has performed the task to which he was called – he has reinstated the ancient languages, thus defrauding godless learning of their crowds of admirers. Perhaps, like

Moses, he will die in the land of Moab, for he is powerless to guide men to those higher studies which lead to divine blessedness. I rejoiced when he ceased expounding the scriptures; for he was not equal to the task. He has done enough in exposing the evils of the Church, but cannot remedy them, or point the way to the promised land. Take my prolixity in good part.

I know you do not need my consolation, for Christ will not forsake you. Pray for me, for I am so occupied with outward things that my health is in as great danger of being injured as my spirit. The monks and nuns who have left their cloisters rob me of many hours, for I am expected to find homes for them all, etc. Farewell, dear Œcolampadius. The grace of Christ be with you! Greet all who are of one mind with us.

MARTIN LUTHER
Currie, 128 *et seq.*

6   To the Christians at Strassburg in Opposition to the Fanatic Spirit

Martin Luther, humble churchman and evangelist at Wittenberg, to the very beloved friends of God, all the Christians at Strassburg.

Grace and peace from God our Father and the Lord Jesus Christ.

Dear sirs and brethren. I greatly rejoice and thank God the Father of mercy for the riches of his grace bestowed upon you, in that he has called you into his wonderful light and let you come into the participation of all the treasures of his Son, Jesus Christ. Now through his salutary Word you can recognize and acknowledge with joyful hearts the true Father, who has redeemed us from the iron furnace of Egyptian sin and death and brought us into the broad, secure, free and verittable Promised Land.

See to it that you do not forget what you previously were, lest you appropriate to yourselves this great grace and mercy without gratitude, as some already have done and fallen again under God's wrath. Remain steadfast, exercise yourselves and increase daily in this knowledge and grace of Jesus Christ (for such is the right road to salvation which will not deceive you). Make it an aim to be of one mind and show brotherly love to each other by your deeds. Thereby your faith will prove itself, instead of being false, worthless, and idle, and the enemy which has been expelled will not return to find the house empty and swept clean and enter with seven evil spirits, so that the last condition will be worse than the first [*Luke* XI: 26].

If on this account you are reviled or persecuted, you are blessed. If they have called the lord of the house Beelzebub, how much more will they do to the children of the household [*Matthew* X: 24, 25]. A servant is not to fare better than his master. And what does it matter if pitiful men who like smoke vanish away [*Psalms* XXXVII: 20] revile you, if you can be assured that myriads of angels in heaven as well as God himself rejoice over you, and with all creatures render thanks and praise for you? All of which your faith and good conscience in the Holy Spirit experience and testify, if indeed you rightly believe and have Christ so that he truly lives and reigns in you. For these sufferings only serve to enrich and foster our blessedness.

But it is perilous when dissension, sects, and errors arise among Christians, for these deprive consciences of such a comforting knowledge, lead to error, and unconsciously turn the spirit from inward grace toward external things and works. Such was the work of false apostles and, after them, of many different kinds of heretics and now, finally, of the Pope. It is of greatest importance that we be on our guard. For if our Gospel is the true Gospel, as I am convinced and have no doubt that it is, then it must naturally follow that it will be attacked, persecuted, and tested from both sides. On the left the opponents will show open contempt and hate, on the right our own will be guilty of dissension and party spirit. 'For', says Paul, 'there must be factions among you in order that those who have stood the test among you may be recognized'. [*I Corinthians* XI: 19]. Christ finds not only Caiphas among his enemies, but also Judas among his friends.

Knowing this, we must be equipped and armed as people who surely must expect at any moment to meet both kinds of attack. We cannot be at all surprised or frightened if dissension arises among us. Instead we must confidently say to ourselves, 'So it will and must be,' and pray God to be with us and keep us on the right path. For, as Moses said, God tests us to know whether or not we depend on him with all our heart [*Deuteronomy* VIII: 2, XIII: 3]. This I say because I have learned how new prophets are appearing in various regions, and, as some of you have written to me, because Dr Karlstadt has started disturbance among you with his fanaticism in the matter of the Sacrament, images and baptism. This he has also done elsewhere, and he blames me for his banishment.

Now my very dear friends, I am not your pastor. No one has to believe me. Each one is responsible for himself. I can warn every one, I can thwart no one. I hope, too, that you have hitherto learned to know me through my writings so that you would admit that in regard to the Gospel, the grace of Christ, the law, faith, love, the cross, human ordinances, our stand towards the Papacy, monasticism, and the Mass, and the articles of faith which a Christian should know, I have written with such clarity and certainty that I am blameless. Nor, I hope, would you deny that, though I am an unworthy instrument of God, he has helped many through me.

Not a single one of these items has been properly treated by Dr Karlstadt, for he has not the ability, as I now can see from his writings. Truly, I never imagined, and at the same time was shocked, to see how deeply he still clings to his errors. As I see his course, he pounces on outward things with such violence, as though the whole strength of the Christian enterprise consisted in the destruction of images, the overthrow of the Sacrament (of the Lord's Supper) and the hindering of baptism. He would like with such smoke and mist to obscure altogether the sun and light of the Gospel and the main articles of Christianity, so that the world might forget everything that we have hitherto taught. Yet he does not come forward to show what in fact is the nature of a true Christian. For it is a mean art, of which any rascal is capable, to destroy images, deny the Sacrament, and decry baptism. This never makes any one a Christian. I must say that he is a coarse devil who hurts me but little.

My sincere counsel and warning is that you be circumspect and hold to the single question, what makes a person a Christian? Do not on any account allow any other question or other art to enjoy equal importance. When anyone proposes anything ask him at once, 'Friend, will this make one a Christian or not?' If not, it cannot be a matter of major importance which requires earnest consideration. If someone is too weak to do this, let him go slowly and wait until he sees what we or others have to say about it. I have hitherto treated fairly and fully of the chief articles of faith. Whoever claims otherwise cannot be a good spirit. I hope that I do no one harm also in the external matters on which these prophets harp so much.

I confess that if Dr Karlstadt, or anyone else, could have convinced me five years ago that only bread and wine were in the sacrament he would have done me a great service. At that time I suffered such severe conflicts and inner strife and torment that I would gladly have been delivered from them. I realized that at this point I could best resist the Papacy. There were two who then wrote me, with much more skill than Dr Karlstadt has, and who did not torture the Word with their own preconceived notions. But I am a captive and cannot free myself. The test is too powerfully present, and will not allow itself to be torn from its meaning by mere verbiage.

Even if someone in these days might try more persuasively to prove that only bread and wine are present, it would not be necessary that he attack me in bitter spirit – which I, unfortunately, am altogether inclined to do, if I assess the nature of the old Adam in me correctly. But the way Dr Karlstadt carries on in this question affects me so little that my position is only fortified the more by him. If I had not previously been of this opinion, such loose, lame, empty talk, set forth on the basis of his own reason and idiosyncrasy without scriptural foundation, would lead me to believe first of all that his opinions amount to nothing. This I hope every one will see, as I give my answer. It is hard for me to believe that he can be serious; if so, God must have hardened his heart and blinded him. For if he were in earnest, he would not have thrown in so many ridiculous passages by wilfully manipulating the Greek and Hebrew languages which, as every one well knows, he has not forgotten to do.

I might well endure his uproar against images, since my writings have done more to overthrow images than he ever will do with his storming and fanaticism. But I will not endure any one inciting and driving Christians to works of this kind, as if one cannot be a Christian without their performance. Nor can we tolerate anyone imprisoning Christian freedom by laws and laying a snare for consciences. For we know that no work can make a Christian, and that such external matters as the use of images and the keeping of the Sabbath are, in the New Testament, as optional as all other ceremonies enjoined by the Law. Paul says, 'We know that an idol has no real existence' [*I Corinthians* VIII: 14]. If so, why then should the Christian conscience be ensnared and tortured on account of something that has no reality? If it has no existence, let it be of no account, whether it falls or stands, as Paul also says about circumcision [*I Corinthians* VII: 19]. But of this we will treat further in our answer.

He blames me for his banishment, and I could endure this if it were true. But this too I will answer in full, if God will. But I am glad that he is out of our land, and I wish he were not among you. It would have been advisable for him to refrain from such an accusation. For I am afraid that clearing myself will mean a severe accusation of him. Beware of the false prophet, whoever can – this is my advice, for no good will come from him. When I met him at Jena he almost convinced me, through a writing of his, not to confuse his spirit with the rebellious and murderous spirit of the Allstedtians. But when, on the order of the prince, I visited his Christians at Orlamünde, I soon found what kind of seed he had sown. I was glad that I wasn't driven out with stones and filth, though some of his people gave me this benediction, 'Get out in the name of a thousand devils, and break your neck before you are out of the city'. This they have of course covered up beautifully in the book they have published about the event. If the ass had horns, that is, if I were prince of Saxony, Dr Karlstadt would not be banished, unless I had been prevailed upon. Under no circumstances ought he to scorn the indulgence of the princes.

But I pray, dear friends, that you might be wiser that we, even though we have become foolish and have written about our actions. I realize well enough that the devil is only seeking opportunities to have us write and read about ourselves, whether we be pious or wicked, so that the main subject of Christ be passed over in silence and the people be made to gape at novelties. Let each one keep his mind on the straight road, for we need all eternity to learn fully about such matters as law, Gospel, faith, the kingdom of Christ, Christian liberty, love, patience and human ordinances. If meanwhile you aren't destroying images, you will not be guilty of sin. Yes, even if you don't receive the Sacrament, you can yet be saved through the Word and faith. The devil has as his main purpose to turn our eyes in this perilous night away from our lamp and lead us off our path by his flying brands and flames.

Ask your evangelists, my dear sirs and brothers, to turn you away from Luther and Karlstadt and direct you always to Christ, but not, as Karlstadt does, only to the work of Christ, wherein Christ is held up as an example, which is the least important aspect of Christ, and which makes him comparable to other saints. But turn to Christ as to a gift of God, or, as Paul says, the power of God, and God's wisdom, righteousness, redemption and sanctification, given to us. For such matters these prophets have little sympathy, taste, or understanding. Instead they juggle with their 'living voice from heaven', their 'laying off the material', 'sprinkling', 'mortification', and similar high-sounding words, which they themselves never understood. They make for confused, disturbed, anxious consciences, and want people to be amazed at their great skill, but meanwhile Christ is forgotten.

Dear brethren, pray that God the Father may keep us from falling into temptation, and may strengthen us according to his unfathomable mercy, preserve us and complete the work he has begun in us. For we have the comfort of being admonished to pray for this through Christ our Saviour. This is an advantage we have over these prophets. For I

E

know and am certain that they have never prayed to God the Father or sought him in initiating their movement; nor do they have a sufficiently good conscience to dare to implore him for a blessed completion. As they began their enterprise in arrogance, so they rush forward recklessly in search of vain honour until at last they end in disgrace. The grace of God be with you all. Amen.

Amer. Edn., XL, 65 et seq.

7   Against the Heavenly Prophets, 1525

Herewith an answer has been given to several of Dr Karlstadt's books. We shall now give our attention to the book which has to do with the Mass, so that we may deal specifically with the Sacrament. For I do not know why he makes so many books, all of which deal with the same subject. He could well put on one page what he wastes on ten. Perhaps he likes to hear himself talk, as the stork its own clattering. For his writing is neither clear nor intelligible, and one would just as soon make one's way through brambles and bushes as read through his books. This is a sign of the spirit. The Holy Spirit speaks well, clearly, in an orderly and distinct fashion. Satan mumbles and chews words in his mouth and makes a hundred into a thousand. It is an effort to ascertain what he means. . . .

Observe carefully, my brother, this order, for everything depends on it. However cleverly this factious spirit makes believe that he regards highly the Word and Spirit of God and declaims passionately about love and zeal for the truth and righteousness of God, he nevertheless has as his purpose to reverse this order. His insolence leads him to set up a contrary order and, as we have said, seeks to subordinate God's outward order to an inner spiritual one. Casting this order to the wind with ridicule and scorn, he wants to get to the Spirit first. Will a handful of water, he says, make me clean from sin? The Spirit, the Spirit, the Spirit,[1] must do this inwardly. Can bread and wine profit me? Will breathing over the bread bring Christ in the sacrament? No, no, one must eat the flesh of Christ spiritually. The Wittenbergers are ignorant of this. They make faith depend on the letter. Whoever does not know the devil might be misled by these many splendid words to think that five holy spirits were in the possession of Karlstadt and his followers.

But should you ask how one gains access to this same lofty spirit they do not refer you to the outward gospel but to some imaginary realm,

[1] A reference to Karlstadt's repeated use of the term.

saying: Remain in 'Self-abstraction' where I now am and you will have the same experience. A heavenly voice will come, and God himself will speak to you. If you inquire further as to the nature of this 'self-abstraction', you will find that they know as much about it as Dr Karlstadt knows of Greek and Hebrew. Do you not see here the devil, the enemy of God's order? With all his mouthing of the words, 'Spirit, Spirit, Spirit', he tears down the bridge, the path, the way, the ladder, and all the means by which the Spirit might come to you. Instead of the outward order of God in the material sign of baptism and the oral proclamation of the Word of God, he wants to teach you, not how the Spirit comes to you but how you come to the Spirit. They would have you learn how to journey on the clouds and ride on the wind. They do not tell you how or when, whither or what, but you are to experience what they do.

Amer. Edn., XL, 118, 146 *et seq.*

O   THE PEASANT WAR

The Peasant War in Germany, 1524-5, was a series of sporadic risings such as had occurred in South Germany and Austria for a century or more. The peasants suffered in a time of quickening economic change, and in the main were concerned to recover lost and concrete liberties, rather than with justice in the abstract or even political rights. In the risings of 1524-5 there were many programmes, and a few manifestos drawn up by lettered men, including one or two clergy among the rebels. Some of these manifestos appealed to Catholic orthodoxy, some to Zwingli, others to the Thuringian reformers, Strauss, Müntzer, Melanchthon and Luther. *The Twelve Articles of the Peasants* (see Kidd, *Documents*, 83) were among the more moderate of these manifestos, and Luther answered them in a tract in which he blamed both sides in the struggle, though he repudiated the concept of a 'Christian revolution' – 'my dear friends, Christians are not so many that they can get together in mobs.' From August 1524 onwards, the rebel bands began to infect other areas and the ferment of revolt spread through the Black Forest area and began to move towards Thuringia in the spring of 1525. Lacking any skilled leadership or planned commissariat, they lived off the land, and from the pillaging of nunneries, monasteries and castles. At first they had great success in the absence of any standing armies among the princes.

They terrorized whole countrysides, and conscripted peasants and sometimes local gentry and whole towns into their cause. It was one of Luther's great counts against them that their bloody revolution endangered the salvation of innocent people, by dragging them into activity which must bring down the judgement of God. In Thuringia the fiery preacher Thomas Müntzer incited the rebels from Mühlhausen and attempted to join forces with the South German rebels. But Philip of Hesse cut them off in the pass at Fulda and moved to join with the forces of Duke George of Saxony. The Thuringian rebels were surrounded at Frankenhausen by Protestant and Catholic troops, routed in a few minutes and punished with dreadful severity. Müntzer was executed. At the height of the excitement, Luther married Katherine von Bora (to spite the devil!) and wrote the brutal tract *Against the robbing and murdering hordes of peasants* inciting the princes to strike down the rebels like mad dogs. His tract which had been written at the zenith of peasant power, read differently when published after Frankenhausen and brought on Luther the reproach of many of his friends, of many common people, and of later history. He confined his activity to interceding for some victims of repression. 'I always said', he said later, 'that if the peasants won, the devil would win. If the princes won, it would be victory for the devil's grandmother.'

1   Thomas Müntzer to his Followers in Allstedt, 27 April 1525

The pure fear of God be with you, brothers. What are you still sleeping for, why have you not recognized the will of God – do you think he has abandoned you, is that it? Ah, how often have I told you that God can only reveal himself in this way, in your apparent abandonment. If not, the offering of your broken and contrite hearts must be in vain. And you must then come into another kind of suffering. I tell you again, if you won't suffer for God, then you will be devil's martyrs. So take care, cheer up, do your duty, and stop pandering to those fantastic perverts, those knaves. Get going, and fight the battle of the Lord! It is high time, keep the brethren together so that they do not mock the divine witness, or they will be all destroyed. The whole of Germany, France and the Roman lands are awake – the Master will start his game, and the knaves are for it! At Fulda in Easter week four collegiate churches were destroyed, the peasants in Klettgau and Hegau are up, three thousand strong, and the longer it goes on the more they are. . . . So now On! On! On! – it is time to hunt the knaves down like dogs – On! On! On! – have no mercy even though Esau gives you good words – *Genesis* XXXIII. Do not look at the misery of the godless. They will beg you, will whine and cry like children. But you are to have no mercy, as God commanded through Moses – *Deuteronomy* VII – and has also revealed to us. Get going in the villages and towns, and especially with the miners and the other good fellows. We must sleep no more. . . . And see, as I write, here is a piece of news which has just come in – from Salza – how the good people there have taken Duke George's officer from his castle . . . the peasants of Eichsfeld have turned enemies to their lords and in brief will have none of their favour. Here's an example for you! On! On! On! Time's up! Balthasar and Bartel Krump, Valtin and Bischoff,[1] you lead the dance out on to the floor! . . . On! On! On! Let not your sword grow cold, let it not be blunted. Smite, cling, clang, on the anvil of Nimrod, and cast the tower to the ground. . . . On! On! On! while it is still day – God goes ahead of you, follow, follow, follow – be not fearful, for God is with you, and you shall not be put off by the numbers against you, for it is not your battle but the Lord's. So go to it through God who will strengthen you in the right faith, without any fear of man. . . .

THOMAS MÜNTZER, a servant of God against the godless.

G. Franz: *Müntzer, Schriften v. Briefe*, 454.*

2   Against the Robbing and Murdering Hordes of Peasants, May 1525

In the former book[2] I did not venture to judge the peasants, since they had offered to be set right and to be instructed, and Christ's command, in *Matthew* VII, says that we are not to judge. But before I look around they go on, and, forgetting their offer, they betake themselves to violence, and rob and rage and act like mad dogs. By this it is easy to see what they had in their false minds, and that the pretences which they made in their twelve articles,[3] under the name of the Gospel, were nothing but lies. It is the devil's work that they are at, and in particular it is the work of the archdevil who rules at Mühlhausen,[4] and does nothing else than stir up robbery, murder and bloodshed; as Christ says of him in *John* VIII, 'He was a murderer from the beginning.' Since,

---

[1] The evocation of names, almost rhythmically, recalls the famous description by John Gower (*Confessio Amantis*) of how the Kentish men were rallied by name in 1381:

Watte vocat, cui Thomme venit, neque Symme retardat
Betteque, Gibbe simul, Hykke venire jubent.

[2] *The Admonition to Peace.*

[3] The formal demands made in March 1525 by the Swabian peasants of their rulers (see *Kidd*, Doc. 83).

[4] Thomas Müntzer.

then, these peasants and wretched folk have let themselves be led astray, and do otherwise than they have promised, I too must write of them otherwise than I have written, and begin by setting their sin before them, as God commands Isaiah and Ezekiel, on the chance that some of them may learn to know themselves. Then I must instruct the rulers how they are to conduct themselves in these circumstances.

The peasants have taken on themselves the burden of three terrible sins against God and man, by which they have abundantly merited death in body and soul. In the first place they have sworn to be true and faithful, submissive and obedient, to their rulers, as Christ commands, when he says, 'Render unto Caesar the things that are Caesar's,' and in *Romans* XIII, 'Let everyone be subject unto the higher powers.' Because they are breaking this obedience, and are setting themselves against the higher powers, wilfully and with violence, they have forfeited body and soul, as faithless, perjured, lying, disobedient knaves and scoundrels are wont to do. St. Paul passed this judgement on them in *Romans* XIII when he said, that they who resist the power will bring a judgement upon themselves. This saying will smite the peasants sooner or later, for it is God's will that faith be kept and duty done.

In the second place, they are starting a rebellion, and violently robbing and plundering monasteries and castles which are not theirs, by which they have a second time deserved death in body and soul, if only as highwaymen and murderers. Besides, any man against whom it can be proved that he is a maker of sedition is outside the law of God and Empire, so that the first who can slay him is doing right and well. For if a man is an open rebel every man is his judge and executioner, just as when a fire starts, the first to put it out is the best man. For rebellion is not simple murder, but is like a great fire, which attacks and lays waste a whole land. Thus rebellion brings with it a land full of murder and bloodshed, makes widows and orphans, and turns everything upside down, like the greatest disaster. Therefore let everyone who can, smite, slay and stab, secretly or openly, remembering that nothing can be more poisonous, hurtful or devilish than a rebel. It is just as when one must kill a mad dog; if you do not strike him, he will strike you, and a whole land with you.

In the third place, they cloak this terrible and horrible sin with the Gospel, call themselves 'Christian brethren', receive oaths and homage, and compel people to hold with them to these abominations. Thus they become the greatest of all blasphemers of God and slanderers of his holy Name, serving the devil, under the outward appearance of the Gospel, thus earning death in body and soul ten times over. I have never heard of a more hideous sin. I suspect that the devil feels the Last Day coming and therefore undertakes such an unheard-of-act, as though saying to himself, 'This is the last, therefore it shall be the worst; I will stir up the dregs and knock out the bottom.' God will guard us against him! See what a mighty prince the devil is, how he has the world in his hands and can throw everything into confusion, when he can so quickly catch so many thousands of peasants, deceive them, blind them, harden them and throw them into revolt, and do with them whatever his raging fury undertakes.

It does not help the peasants, when they pretend that, according to *Genesis i* and *ii*, all things were created free and common, and that all of us alike have been baptized. For under the New Testament Moses does not count; for there stands our Master, Christ, and subjects us, with our bodies and our property, to the emperor and the law of this world, when he says, 'Render to Caesar the things that are Caesar's.' Paul, too, says, in *Romans* XII, to all baptized Christians, 'Let every man be subject to the power', and Peter says, 'Be subject to every ordinance of man.' By this doctrine of Christ we are bound to live, as the Father commands from heaven, saying, 'This is My beloved Son; hear him.' For baptism does not make men free in body and property, but in soul; and the Gospel does not make goods common, except in the case of those who do of their own free will what the apostles and disciples did in *Acts* IV. They did not demand, as do our insane peasants in their raging, that the goods of others – of a Pilate and a Herod – should be common, but only their own goods. Our peasants, however, would have other men's goods common, and keep their own goods for themselves. Fine Christians these! I think there is not a devil left in hell; they have all gone into the peasants. Their raving has gone beyond all measure.

Since the peasants, then, have brought both God and man down upon them and are already so many times guilty of death in body and soul, since they submit to no court and wait for no verdict, but only rage on, I must instruct the worldly governors how they are to act in the matter with a clear conscience.

First. I will not oppose a ruler who, even though he does not tolerate the Gospel, will smite and punish these peasants without offering to submit the case to judgement. For he is within his rights, since the peasants are not contending any longer for the Gospel, but have become faithless, perjured, disobedient, rebellious murderers, robbers and blasphemers, whom even heathen rulers have the right and power to punish; nay, it is their duty to punish them, for it is just for this purpose that they bear the sword, and are 'the ministers of God upon him that doeth evil'.

But if the ruler is a Christian and tolerates the Gospel, so that the peasants have no appearance of a case against him, he should proceed with fear. First he must take the matter to God, confessing that we have deserved these things, and remembering that God may, perhaps, have thus aroused the devil as a punishment upon all Germany. Then he should humbly pray for help against the devil, for 'we are battling not only against flesh and blood, but against spiritual wickedness in the air', and this must be attacked with prayer. Then, when our hearts are so turned to God that we are ready to let his divine will be done, whether he will or will not have us to be princes and lords, we must go beyond our duty, and offer the mad peasants an opportunity to come to terms, even though they are not worthy of it. Finally, if that does not help, then swiftly grasp the sword.

For a prince and lord must remember in this case that he is God's minister and the servant of his wrath (*Romans* XIII), to whom the sword is committed for use upon such fellows, and that he sins as greatly against God, if he does not punish and protect and does not fulfil the duties of his office, as does one to whom the sword has not been committed when he commits a murder. If he can punish and does not – even though the punishment consist in the taking of life and the shedding of blood – then he is guilty of all the murder and all the evil which these fellows commit, because, by wilful neglect of the divine command, he permits them to practice their wickedness, though he can prevent it, and is in duty bound to do so. Here, then, there is no time for sleeping; no place for patience or mercy. It is the time of the sword, not the day of grace.

The rulers, then, should go on unconcerned, and with a good conscience lay about them as long as their hearts still beat. It is to their advantage that the peasants have a bad conscience and an unjust cause, and that any peasant who is killed is lost in body and soul and is eternally the devil's. But the rulers have a good conscience and a just cause; and can, therefore, say to God with all assurance of heart, 'Behold, my God, thou hast appointed me prince or lord, of this I can have no doubt; and though hast committed to me the sword over the evildoers (*Romans* XIII). It is thy Word, and cannot lie. I must fulfill my office, or forfeit thy grace. It is also plain that these peasants have deserved death many times over, in thine eyes and the eyes of the world, and have been committed to me for punishment. If it be thy will that I be slain by them, and that my rulership be taken from me and destroyed, so be it: thy

will be done. So shall I die and be destroyed fulfilling thy commandment and thy Word, and shall be found obedient to thy commandment
and my office. Therefore will I punish and smite as long as my heart
beats. Thou wilt judge and make things right.'

Thus it may be that one who is killed fighting on the ruler's side may
be a true martyr in the eyes of God, if he fights with such a conscience
as I have just described, for he is in God's Word and is obedient to him.
On the other hand, one who perishes on the peasants' side is an eternal
brand of hell, for he bears the sword against God's Word and is disobedient to him, and is a member of the devil. And even though it
happens that the peasants gain the upper hand (which God forbid!) –
for to God all things are possible, and we do not know whether it may
be his will, through the devil, to destroy all order and rule and cast the
world upon a desolate heap, as a prelude to the Last Day, which cannot
be far off – nevertheless, they may die without worry and go to the
scaffold with a good conscience, who are found exercising their office
of the sword. They may leave to the devil the kingdom of the world,
and take in exchange the everlasting kingdom. Strange times, these,
when a prince can win heaven with bloodshed, better than other men
with prayer!

Finally, there is another thing that ought to move the rulers. The
peasants are not content to be themselves the devil's own, but they
force and compel many good people against their wills to join their
devilish league, and so make them partakers of all of their own wickedness and damnation. For anyone who consents to what they do, goes
to the devil with them, and is guilty of all the evil deeds that they commit; though he has to do this because he is so weak in faith that he does
not resist them. A pious Christian ought to suffer a hundred deaths,
rather than give a hair's breadth of consent to the peasants' cause. O
how many martyrs could now be made by the bloodthirsty peasants
and the murdering prophets! Now the rulers ought to have mercy on
these prisoners of the peasants, and if they had no other reason to use
the sword, with a good conscience, against the peasants, and to risk
their own lives and property in fighting them, there would be reason
enough, and more than enough, in this – that thus they would be rescuing and helping these souls, whom the peasants have forced into
their devilish league and mho, without willing it, are sinning so hor-
ribly, and who must be damned. For truly these souls are in purgatory;
nay, in the bonds of hell and the devil.

Therefore, dear lords, here is a place where you can release, rescue,
help. Have mercy on these poor people [whom the peasants have com-

pelled to join them]. Stab, smite, slay, whoever can. If you die in doing
it, well for you! A more blessed death can never be yours, for you die
in doing it, well for you! A more blessed death can never be yours, for
you die in obeying the divine Word and commandment in *Romans* XIII,
and in loving service of your neighbour, whom you are rescuing from
the bonds of hell and of the devil. And so I beg everyone who can to
flee from the peasants as from the devil himself; those who do not flee,
I pray that God will enlighten and convert. As for those who are not to
be converted, God grant that they may have neither fortune nor success.
To this let every pious Christian say Amen! For this prayer is right and
good, and pleases God; this I know. If anyone think this too hard, let
him remember that rebellion is intolerable and that the destruction of
the world is to be expected every hour.

Philad. Edn., IV, 248 *et seq.*

3   To Rühel, 23 May 1525

At the height of the Peasant War Luther's patron-protector, Frederick the
Wise, died.

My gracious lord departed this life in the enjoyment of his full reason,
taking the sacrament in both kinds and without supreme unction. We
buried him without Masses or vigils, but yet in a fine noble manner.
Several stones were found in his lungs and three (wonderful to relate)
in his gall; in fact he died of the stone. . . . The signs of his death were
a rainbow which Melanchthon and I saw one night last winter over
Lochau, and a child born here at Wittenberg without a head, and another with feet turned around.

MARTIN LUTHER
Smith, *Life and Letters*, 163-4

4   To Leonard Koppe of Torgau, 17 June 1525

Grace and peace in Christ! I wish you to read this very depressing letter,
honoured sir, to see if you know of no one who could help in this
matter, for it is too much to expect one in your high position to do so.
If you know of neon, then return the letter, so that I may seek help
elsewhere, for I am quite unhappy about the two children.

Most worthy Father Prior, you know what has happened to me –

that the nun that with God's help you carried off from the nunnery two years ago is nevertheless returning to the cloister, not this time, however, to take the veil, but as the honoured wife of Dr Luther, who, up till now, has lived alone in the old empty monastery of St. Augustine at Wittenberg. So pray come to my home-coming, which is on the Tuesday after St. John's festival, but without any wedding present.

MARTIN LUTHER
Currie, 140 *et seq.*

5 To Desiderius Erasmus at Basel, Wittenberg ([?] 15 April 1524)

Grace and peace from our Lord Jesus Christ. I have been silent long enough, excellent Erasmus, having waited for you, as the greater and elder man, to speak first; but as you refuse to do so, I think that charity itself now compels me to begin. I say nothing about your estrangement from us, by which you were made safer against my enemies the Papists. Nor do I especially resent your action, intended to gain their favour or mitigate their hostility, in censuring and attacking us in various books. For since we see that the Lord has not given you courage or sense to assail those monsters openly and confidently with us, we are not the men to exact what is beyond your power and measure. Rather we have tolerated and even respected the mediocrity of God's gift in you. The whole world knows your services to letters and how you have made them flourish and thus prepared a path for the direct study of the Bible. For this glorious and splendid gift in you we ought to thank God. I for one have never wished you to leave your little sphere to join our camp, for although you might have profited the cause much by your ability, genius and eloquence, yet as you had not the courage it was safer for you to work at home. We only fear that you might be induced by our enemies to fall upon our doctrine with some publication, in which case we should be obliged to resist you to your face. We have restrained some who would have drawn you into the arena, and have even suppressed books already written against you. We should have preferred that Hutten's *Expostulation* had not been written, and still more that your *Sponge* had not seen the light. Incidentally I may remark, that, unless I mistake, when you wrote that book you felt how easy it is to write about moderation and blame Luther's excesses, but how hard or rather impossible it is to practise what you preach except by a special gift of the Spirit. Believe it or not as you like, but Christ is witness that I heartily regret that such zeal and hatred should be roused against you. I cannot believe that you remain unmoved by it, for your fortitude is human and unequal to such trials. Perhaps a righteous zeal moved them and they thought that you have provoked them in various ways. Since they are admittedly too weak to bear your caustic but dissembled sarcasm (which you would have pass for prudent moderation), they surely have a just cause for indignation, whereas if they were stronger they would have none. I, too, am irritable, and quite frequently am moved to write caustically, though I have only done so against hardened men proof against milder forms of admonition. Otherwise I think my gentleness and clemency towards sinners, no matter how far they are gone in iniquity, is witnessed not only by my own conscience but by the experience of many. Hitherto, accordingly, I have controlled my pen as often as you prick me, and have written in letters to friends which you have seen that I would control it until you publish something openly. For although you will not side with us and although you injure or make sceptical many pious persons by your impiety and hypocrisy, yet I cannot and do not accuse you of wilful obstinacy. What can I do? Each side is greatly exasperated. Could my good offices prevail, I would wish my friends to cease attacking you with so much animus and to allow your old age a peaceful death in the Lord. I think they would do so if they were reasonable and considered your weakness and the greatness of the cause which has long since outgrown your littleness, especially as the cause has now progressed so far that it has little to fear from the might – or rather the sting and bite – of Erasmus. You on your side, Erasmus, ought to consider their infirmity and abstain from making them the butt of your witty rhetoric. Even if you cannot and dare not declare for us, yet at least you might leave us alone and mind your own business. If they suffer from your bites, *you* certainly will confess that human weakness has cause to fear the name and fame of Erasmus and that it is a very much graver matter to be snapped at by you than to be ground to pieces by all the papists together. I say this, excellent Erasmus, as an evidence of my *candid moderation*, wishing that the Lord might give you a spirit worthy of your reputation, but if he delays doing so I beg that meanwhile if you can do nothing else you will remain a spectator of the conflict and not join our enemies, and especially that you publish no book against me, as I shall write none against you. Remember that the men who are called Lutherans are human beings like ourselves, whom you ought to spare and forgive as Paul says: 'Bear ye one another's burdens.' We have fought long enough, we must take care not to eat each other up. This would be a terrible catastrophe, as neither one of us really wishes harm to religion, and without judging each other both may do good. Pardon my poor style and farewell in the Lord. . . .

MARTIN LUTHER
Smith, *Life and Letters*, 204 *et seq.*

6   From 'De Servo Arbitrio', 'On the Will as Unfree', 1525. The 'Internal' and 'External' Clarity of Scripture

. . . I admit, of course, that there are many texts in the scriptures that are obscure and abstruse, not because of the majesty of their subject-matter, but because of our ignorance of their vocabulary and grammar; but these texts in no way hinder a knowledge of all the subject-matter of scripture. For what still sublimer thing can remain hidden in the scriptures, now that the seals have been broken, the stone rolled from the door of the sepulchre, and the supreme mystery brought to light, namely that Christ the Son of God has been made man, that God is three and one, that Christ has suffered for us and is to reign eternally? Are not these things known and sung even in the highways and byways? Take Christ out of the scriptures and what will you find left in them?

The subject-matter of the scriptures, therefore, is all quite accessible, even though some texts are still obscure owing to our ignorance of their terms. Truly it is stupid and impious when we know that the subject-matter of scripture has all been placed in the clearest light, to call it obscure on account of a few obscure words. If the words are obscure in one place, yet they are plain in another; and it is one and the same theme, published quite openly to the whole world, which in the scriptures is sometimes expressed in plain words, and sometimes lies as yet hidden in obscure words. Now, when the thing signified is in the light, it does not matter if this or that sign of it is in darkness, since many other signs of the same thing are meanwhile in the light. Who will say that a public fountain is not in the light, because those who are in a narrow side-street do not see it, whereas all who are in the market-place do see it?

Your reference to the Corycian cave, therefore, is irrelevant; that is not how things are in the scriptures. Matters of the highest majesty and the profoundest mysteries are no longer hidden away, but have been brought out and are openly displayed before the very doors. For Christ has opened our minds so that we may understand the scriptures, and the Gospel is preached to the whole creation; 'their voice has gone out to all the earth', and 'whatever was written was written for our instruction'; also, 'all scripture inspired by God is profitable for teaching'. See, then, whether you and all the sophists can produce any single mystery that is still abstruse in the scriptures.

It is true that for many people much reamins abstruse; but this is not due to the obscurity of scripture, but to the blindness or indolence of those who will not take the trouble to look at the very clearest truth. It is as Paul says of the Jews in *II Corinthians* [III:15], 'a veil lies over their minds'; and again, 'if our gospel is veiled, it is veiled only to those who are perishing, whose minds the god of this world has blinded' [*II Corinthians* IV:3 *et seq.*]. With similar temerity a man might veil his own eyes, or go out of the light into the darkness and hide himself, and then blame the sun and the day for being obscure. Let miserable men, therefore, stop imputing the darkness and obscurity of their own hearts, with blasphemous perversity, to the wholly clear scriptures of God. . . .

To put it briefly, there are two kinds of clarity in scripture, just as there are also two kinds of obscurity: one external and pertaining to the ministry of the Word, the other located in the understanding of the heart. If you speak of the internal clarity, no man perceives one iota of what is in the scriptures unless he has the Spirit of God. All men have a darkened heart so that even if they can recite everything in scripture, and know how to quote it, yet they apprehend and truly understand nothing of it. They neither believe in God, nor that they themselves are creatures of God, nor anything else, *Psalm* [XIV:1] says, 'The fool has said in his heart, "There is no God."' For the Spirit is required for the understanding of scripture, both as a whole and in any part of it. If, on the other hand, you speak of the external clarity, nothing at all is left obscure or ambiguous, but everything there is in the scriptures has been brought out by the Word into the most definite light, and published to all the world. . . .

What we say is this: the spirits are to be tested or proved by two sorts of judgement. One is internal, whereby through the Holy Spirit or a special gift of God, anyone who is enlightened concerning himself and his own salvation, judges and discerns with the greatest certainty the dogmas and opinions of all men. Of this it is said in *I Corinthians* [II:15]: 'The spiritual man judges all things, but himself is judged by no one.' This belongs to faith and is necessary for every individual

Christian. We have called it above 'the internal clarity of holy scripture'. Perhaps this was what those had in mind who gave you the reply that everything must be decided by the judgement of the Spirit. But this judgement helps no one else, and with it we are not here concerned; for no one, I think, doubts its reality.

There is therefore another, an external judgement, whereby with the greatest certainty we judge the spirits and dogmas of all men, not only for ourselves, but also for others and for their salvation. This judgement belongs to the public ministry of the Word and to the outward office, and is chiefly the concern of leaders and preachers of the Word. We make use of it when we seek to strengthen those who are weak in faith and confute opponents. This is what we earlier called 'the external clarity of holy scripture'. Thus we say that all spirits are to be tested in the presence of the Church at the bar of scripture. For it ought above all to be settled and established among Christians that the holy scriptures are a spiritual light far brighter than the sun itself, especially in things that are necessary to salvation. But because we have for so long been persuaded of the opposite by that pestilential saying of the sophists that the scriptures are obscure and ambiguous, we are obliged to begin by proving even that first principle of ours by which everything else has to be proved – a procedure which among the philosophers would be regarded as absurd and impossible. . . .

W.A., XVIII, 606-9, 653*; Rupp and Drewery, 1970.

PART V *From Luther to Lutheranism, 1526-1535*

P THE EUCHARISTIC CONTROVERSY AND THE MARBURG COLLOQUY

For political as well as religious reasons, Philip of Hesse in Germany and Zwingli in Switzerland were anxious to heal the widening breach between Luther and the Swiss concerning the eucharist. The result was the colloquy at Marburg, October 1529. Neither side would compromise. Luther held to his simple Biblicism, affirming that 'This is my body' implied a real presence. Zwingli and Œcolampadius championed a true, spiritual presence. Despite agreement on other matters, and despite a growth in understanding, agreement was not reached and the reformers departed, unable to give one another the hand of friendship.

1 That these words of Christ, 'This is my body', etc., still stand firm against the fanatics, 1527

It is precisely the same devil who now assails us through the fanatics by blaspheming the holy and venerable sacrament of our Lord Jesus Christ, out of which they would like to make mere bread and wine as a symbol or memorial sign of Christians, in whatever way their dream or fancy dictates. They will not grant that the Lord's body and blood are present, even though the plain, clear words stand right there: 'Eat, this is my body.' Yet those words still stand firm and invulnerable against them. . .

Let us take up the saying of Christ, which Matthew and Mark record: 'He took bread, and gave thanks, and broke it, and gave it to his

disciples and said, "Take, eat; this is my body which is given for you."'
. . . Now, here stands the text, stating clearly and lucidly that Christ
gives his body to eat when he distributes the bread. On this we take
our stand, and we also believe and teach that in the Supper we eat and
take to ourselves Christ's body truly and physically. But how this takes
place or how he is in the bread, we do not know and are not meant to
know. God's Word we should believe without setting bounds or
measure to it. The bread we see with our eyes, but we hear with our
ears that Christ's body is present. . . .

But listen, I ask you, how they remove our interpretation from this
saying of Christ and bring in their own. They say, 'The word "is"
must mean the same as the word "represents"', as Zwingli writes; and
the expression 'my body' must mean the same as the expression 'sign
of my body', as Œcolampadius writes. So Christ's Word and meaning
according to Zwingli's text would read, 'Take, eat; this represents my
body', or according to Œcolampadius' text, 'Take and eat; this is a
sign of my body.' . . . Then at once they boast that we have no passage
from scripture which says that Christ's body is in the Supper. . . .

Whoever read in the scriptures that 'body' means the same as 'sign
of the body', and 'is' means the same as 'represents'? Indeed, what language in all the world has ever expressed itself so?

There is no proof of representation, either, in all the other passages
which they quote. For example, where Christ says, 'I am the true vine'
[*John* xv:1], he speaks of the true spiritual vine, which he also *was*, not
which *represents* him. How should it read: 'I represent the true vine,'
or, 'I am represented by the true vine'? Who then is the true vine, apart
from any representation? Again, 'I am the shepherd' (*John* x:11), 'I am
the door' (*John* x:7), 'I am the resurrection and the life' (*John* xi:25),
and all the others. All these sayings are expressed and understood in
terms of being, not of representing. . . .

This bread in the Supper is his body, which he made as God who
makes all bodies and calls them his bodies; moreover, he ordains this
to be his body with the intention that it should be his body in a new
manner – to be eaten in remembrance of him. Thus the bread should be
called his body for two reasons, first on account of the creation, secondly
on account of the ordinance, in opposition to Moses and the body of
the paschal lamb in the Old Testament, in which he calls the same bread
his body, in other words, a body for his use. Just as I call a knife 'my
iron', or a coat 'my cloth', on account of their use, although not I but
God alone made them in respect to their substance, and not I but the
smith or tailor made them in respect to their form. So too, Christ can

easily call the bread his body, since he has made and now uses this body for his own purpose. . . .

Bread and wine are eaten and drunk for the forgiveness of sins; that is, because Christ ordained them to be eaten and drunk in order to keep his remembrance, it is proper to call this an eating and drinking of the forgiveness of sins, since in connection with it we should remember that forgiveness and do as he says afterward, 'Do this in remembrance of me.' Just as one drinks wine to seal a sale, to show that it was a fair and just transaction which should be kept in remembrance and honoured. . . .

We take up the article that Christ sits at the right hand of God, which the fanatics maintain makes it impossible for Christ's body also to be in the Supper. . . .

The scriptures teach us, however, that the right hand of God is not a specific place in which a body must or may be, such as on a golden throne, but is the almighty power of God, which at one and the same time can be nowhere and yet must be everywhere. It cannot be at any one place, I say. . . .

On the other hand, it must be essentially present at all places, even in the tiniest tree leaf. The reason is this: it is God who creates, effects and preserves all things through his almighty power and right hand, as our creed confesses. For he dispatches no officials or angels when he creates or preserves something, but all this is the work of his divine power itself. If he is to create or preserve it, however, he must be present and must make and preserve his creation both in its innermost and outermost aspects. . . .

Their second chief argument is the saying of *John* VI [:63], 'Flesh is of no avail,' which Œcolampadius boasts of as his iron wall. In truth, he needs a good one! . . .

We maintain both the physical and the spiritual eating. The mouth eats the body of Christ physically, for it cannot grasp or eat the words, nor does it know what it is eating. As far as taste is concerned the mouth surely seems to be eating something other than Christ's body. But the heart grasps the words in faith and eats spiritually precisely the same body as the mouth eats physically, for the heart sees very well what the uncomprehending mouth eats physically. But how does it see this? Not by looking at the bread or at the mouth's eating, but at the word which is there, 'Eat, this is my body.' Yet there is only one body of Christ, which both mouth and heart eat, each in its own mode and manner. The heart cannot eat it physically nor can the mouth eat it spiritually. So God arranges that the mouth eats physically for the heart and the heart eats spiritually for the mouth, and thus both are satisfied and saved by one and the same food. . . .

Amer. Edn., XXXVII, 18 et seq.

2   Philip of Hesse to Zwingli, 22 April 1529

We are presently attempting to call together Luther and Melanchthon, as well as those who share your views concerning the sacrament. Perhaps the gracious and almighty God will bestow his grace so that on the basis of the sacred scriptures concord can be achieved concerning this article which would enable us to live in common Christian understanding. At this Diet the Papists attempt to support their false life and morals by insisting that we, who adhere to the pure and clear Word of God, are not of one accord concerning our faith. Thus I graciously request that you will eagerly do your part to bring together at an appointed time and place both you and the Lutherans so that, as I said before, the matter can rightly be brought to a Christian consensus.

Hillerbrand, 152

3   From Bullinger's Account of Marburg, October 1529

Zwingli set out on 3 September alone, except for Rudolf Collium (professor of Greek at Zürich) and made his way to Basel so quietly that nobody except the secret Council knew anything about it. But on the next day his journey and the reason for it were made public, and an official of the Council was sent after him with Ulrich Funk and a servant, together with guards. . . .

Wondrous rumours began to be spread about Zwingli in the Confederacy. Some said he had run away with a band of rogues. Others said the devil had come to him visibly and whisked him away. Similar rumours – equally extravagant and worthless – were spread without number. In Basel Zwingli joined forces with Johann Œcolampadius and an official of the Council, and went on to Strasbourg, where he was honourably received and preached a sermon with universal applause. . . .

At Strasbourg he was joined by Martin Bucer and Dr. Caspar Hedio and several officials of the Council, and they went on to Marburg. They were accompanied by Jacob Sturm, Counsel of Strasbourg and Jacob von Dukenheim, a lord or nobleman from Meissen, whom the Landgrave had appointed for this duty. At Marburg they met with a cordial reception from the authorities.

Dr Martin Luther arrived later. He had lingered for some time in Saxon territory, waiting till the escort from the Landgrave arrived to take him on from there, for he did not wish to leave Saxony without this protection. The Landgrave passed the remark that 'Zwingli and his company came from Switzerland without an escort, but Dr Luther demanded one, as if he trusted us less.' With Luther there came Philip Melanchthon and Justus Jonas from Saxony, Stephen Agricola from Augsburg, Andreas Osiander from Nuremberg and Johann Brenz from Schwäbisch Hall.

Other learned men came from many countries to hear the colloquy between these eminent and famous men, but only a few were admitted. The Landgrave laid down at the start that some of those who had been invited should have private discussions together, and specifically named Luther with Œcolampadius and Zwingli with Melanchthon. It was thought useless for Luther and Zwingli – both of them vehement and hot-tempered – to meet at the opening stage; Œcolampadius and Melanchthon were more gracious and gentle, and were each asked to talk with one of the more violent ones.

Zwingli and Melanchthon discussed in particular the deity of Christ, original sin, the Word of God, the Sacrament of our Lord's Supper. . . . Such also was the content of the discussion between Luther and Œcolampadius. . . .

Bullinger, Reformationsgeschichte, II, 224-6*

4   To Katherine Luther at Wittenberg, 4 October 1529

Grace and peace in Christ. Dear Lord, Katie, know that our friendly conference at Marburg is now at an end and that we are in perfect union in all points except that out opponents insist that there is simply bread and wine in the Lord's Supper, and that Christ is only in it in a spiritual sense. Today the Landgrave did his best to make us united, hoping that even though we disagreed yet we should hold each other as brothers and members of Christ. He worked hard for it, but we would not call them brothers or members of Christ, although we wish them well and desire to remain at peace. I think tomorrow or day after we shall depart to go and see the Elector at Scheitz in Vogtland, whither he has summoned us.

Tell Bugenhagen that Zwingli's best argument was that a body could not exist without occupying space and therefore Christ's body was not in the bread, and that Œcolampadius' best argument was that the Sacrament is only the sign of Christ's body. I think God blinded them that they could not get beyond these points. I have much to do and the messenger is in a hurry. Say good-night to all and pray for me. We are all sound and well and live like princes. Kiss little Lena and Hans for me.

> Your humble servant, MARTIN LUTHER
> Smith, *Life and Letters*, 245

5   To Nicholas Gerbel at Strassburg, Marburg, 4 October 1529

Grace and peace in Christ. You will know, my dear Gerbel, how far we attained harmony at Marburg, partly by the verbal report of your representatives, partly by the Articles they are taking with them. We defended ourselves strongly and they conceded much, but as they were firm in this one Article of the sacrament of the altar we dismissed them in peace, fearing that further argument would draw blood. We ought to have charity and peace even with our foes, and so we plainly told them, that unless they grow wiser on this point they may indeed have our charity, but cannot by us be considered as brothers and members of Christ. You will judge how much fruit has come of this conference; it seems to me that no small scandal has been removed, since there will be no further occasion for disputation, which is more than we had hoped for. Would that the little difference still remaining might be taken away by Christ. Farewell, brother, and pray for me.

> Yours, MARTIN LUTHER
> Smith, *Life and Letters*, 245 et seq.

6   Zwingli to Vadian, 20 October 1529

Grace and peace to you from the Lord.

I'll give you a brief account of what you are so anxious to learn. When we had been brought to Marburg under most trusty escort, and Luther had arrived with his own friends, the Landgrave decided that there should be separate preliminary conferences in private, Œcolampadius with Luther and Melanchthon with Zwingli, to seek between themselves for any possible measure of agreement that could lead to peace. Here Luther's reaction to Œcolampadius was such that he came to me and privately complained that once again he'd come up against Eck! Don't tell this to anyone you can't trust. Melanchthon I found uncommonly slippery; he kept changing his shape like another Proteus, forced me – in lieu of salt! – to use my pen as a weapon and keep my hand dry, so that I could hold him fast for all his chafings and wrigglings and dodgings. I am sending you a copy of a few extracts from our very lengthy conversations on the understanding that you will only show it to those you can trust – I mean, to those who will not use it to stir up another crisis: remember that Philip has a copy too, for I drew it up in his presence and under his eye, and many of his own words he actually dictated. But the last thing we want is to bring on a new crisis. Philip and I spent six hours together, Luther and Œcolampadius three.

On the next day the four of us entered the arena in the presence of the Landgrave and a few others – twenty-four at most; we fought it out in this and in three further sessions, thus making four in all in which, with witnesses, we fought our winning battle. Three times we threw at Luther the fact that he had at other times given a different exposition from the one he was now insisting on of those ridiculous ideas of his, that Christ suffered in his divine nature, that the body of Christ is everywhere, and that the flesh profits nothing; but the dear man had nothing to say in reply – except that on the matter of the flesh profiting nothing he said: 'You know, Zwingli, that all the ancient writers have again and again changed their interpretations of passages of scripture as time went on and their judgement matured.' He said: 'The body of Christ is eaten and received into our body in the bodily sense (*corporaliter*), but at the same time I reserve my judgement on whether the human spirit eats his body too' – when a little before he had said :'the body of Christ is eaten by the mouth in the bodily sense, but the human spirit does not eat him in the bodily sense.' He said: '[the bread and wine] are made into the body of Christ by the utterance of these words – "This is my body" – however great a criminal the one might be who pronounces them.' He conceded that the body of Christ is finite. He conceded that the Eucharist may be called a 'sign' of the body of Christ. These are examples of the countless inconsistencies, the absurdities and follies which he bleats out like a babbling beach; but we refuted him so successfully that the Landgrave himself has now come down on our side, though he does not say so in the presence of some of the princes. The Hessian entourage, almost to a man, has withdrawn from Luther's position. The Landgrave himself has given permission for our books to

be read with impunity, and in future will not allow bishops who share
our views to be ejected from their place. John, the Saxon prince, was
not there, but [Ulrich of] Württemberg was.

We left Marburg with certain agreements which you will soon see
in writing. The truth prevailed so manifestly that if ever a man was
beaten in this world, it was Luther – for all his impudence and obstinacy
– and everyone witnessed it, too, although of course the judge was dis-
creet and impartial. Even so, Luther kept on exclaiming that he hadn't
been beaten etc. We have, however, achieved this much good, that our
agreement on the rest of the doctrines of the Christian religion will
preclude the Papal party from hoping any longer that Luther will come
over to them.

I'm still tired from my journey as I write. When you come here,
you'll be told everything in detail. For I believe that we've achieved
some other things that will make for the protection of our religion and
against the autocracy of the Emperor. When the right time comes, they
will have to be explained to you as well.

Meanwhile, farewell, and give my greetings to all our friends.

Your own, ULRICH ZWINGLI*

Q   LUTHER'S TWO CATECHISMS

Luther's two catechisms were intended to meet two urgent needs, for a manual
of instruction for Christian teachers, and for a direct and simple instrument for
catechizing Christians. The first he met in his larger Catechism, 1529, the second
in a slender document of classic simplicity and enduring impact. It deals with
the Commandments, Creed, Lord's Prayer and Sacraments, and we print the
exposition of the Creed.

1   Luther's Short Catechism, July 1529

PREFACE

Martin Luther to all faithful, pious pastors, and preachers: Grace,
mercy, and peace in Jesus Christ our Lord.

In setting forth this Catechism or Christian doctrine in such a simple, concise, and easy form, I have been compelled and driven by the wretched and lamentable state of affairs which I discovered lately when I acted as inspector. Merciful God, what misery I have seen, the common people knowing nothing at all of Christian doctrine – especially in the villages! – and unfortunately many pastors are wellnigh unskilled and incapable of teaching; and though all are called Christians and partake of the Holy Sacrament, they know neither the Lord's Prayer, nor the Creed, nor the Ten Commandments, but live like the poor cattle and senseless swine, though, now that the Gospel is come, they have learnt well enough how they may abuse their liberty.

O ye bishops, how will ye ever answer for it to Christ that ye have so shamefully neglected the people and have not attended for an instant to your office? May all evil be averted from you! Ye forbid the taking of the Sacrament in one kind, and insist on your human laws, but never inquire whether they know the Lord's Prayer, the Creed, the Ten Commandments, or any of the words of God. Oh, woe upon you for evermore!

Therefore I pray you for God's sake, my good masters and brethren who are pastors or preachers, to attend to your office with all your heart, to take pity on your people, who are commended to your charge, and to help us to introduce the Catechism among the people, especially among the young; and let those who cannot do better take these tables and forms, and instruct the people in them word for word; . . .

When thou hast taught them this short Catechism, then take the larger Catechism, and give them a deeper and fuller explanation. Explain every commandment, petition and article, with its various works and uses, its dangers and abuses, as thou wilt find them in abundance in the many little books written about them. And especially dwell on that commandment that is most neglected among thy people. For example, the Seventh Commandment, about stealing, must be vehemently urged among artisans, tradesmen, and also among peasants and servants, for among such people there is all manner of unfaithfulness and thieving. Again the Fourth Commandment must be especially urged upon children and the common people, that they may be quiet, faithful, obedient, peaceful; and thou must always adduce many examples from the Bible of how God punished or blessed such people. . . .

THE CREED

How the master of the house is to explain it as simply as possible to his household.

The First Article: of the Creation

I believe in God the Father Almighty, Maker of heaven and earth.

What does that mean?

ANSWER: I believe that God has created me and all other creatures, and has given me, and preserves for me, body and soul, eyes, ears, and all my limbs, my reason and all my senses; and that daily he bestows on me clothes and shoes, meat and drink, house and home, wife and child, fields and cattle, and all my goods, and supplies in abundance all needs and necessities of my body and life, and protects me from all perils, and guards and defends me from all evil. And this he does out of pure fatherly and divine goodness and mercy, without any merit or worthiness in me; for all which I am bound to thank him and praise him, and, moreover, to serve and obey him. This is a faithful saying.

The Second Article: of the Redemption

And in Jesus Christ, his only Son, our Lord, who was conceived by the Holy Ghost, born of the Virgin Mary; suffered under Pontius Pilate; was crucified, dead, and buried, he descended into hell; the third day he rose again from the dead; he ascended into heaven, and sitteth at the right hand of the Father Almighty; from thence he shall come to judge the quick and the dead.

What does that mean?

ANSWER: I believe that Jesus Christ, very God, born of the Father in eternity, and aslo very man, born of the Virgin Mary is my Lord, who has redeemed me, a lost and damned man, and has won and delivered me from all sins, from death, and from the power of the devil, not with gold and silver, but with his holy and precious blood and with his innocent passion and death, so that I might be his own, and might live under him in his kingdom, and serve him in everlasting righteousness, innocence, and blessing, just as he rose from the dead, and lives and reigns in all eternity. This is a faithful saying.

The Third Article: of the Sanctification

I believe in the Holy Ghost, a holy Christian Church, the communion of saints, the forgiveness of sins, the resurrection of the body, and the life everlasting. Amen.

What does that mean?

ANSWER: I believe that I cannot of my own understanding and strength believe in or come to Jesus Christ my Lord, but that the Holy Ghost has called me by the Gospel, and illuminated me with his gifts, and sanctfied and preserved me in the true faith, just as he calls, gathers together, illuminates, sanctifies and preserves in Jesus Christ all Christendom throughout the earth in the one true faith; in which Christendom he daily bestows abundantly on me and all believers forgiveness of sins; and on the last day he will awaken me and all the dead, and will give to me and all that believe in Christ eternal life. This is a faithful saying....

Kidd, Doc., 97

2   A Hymn of Luther

A safe stronghold our God is still,
A trusty shield and weapon,
He'll help us clear from all the ill
That hath us now o'ertaken.
The ancient prince of hell
Hath risen with purpose fell;
Strong mail of craft and power
He weareth in this hour;
On earth is not his fellow.

With force of arms we nothing can,
Full soon were we down-ridden;
But for us fights the proper Man,
Whom God himself hath bidden.
Ask ye: Who is this same?
Christ Jesus is his name,
The Lord Sabaoth's Son;
He, and no other one,
Shall conquer in the battle.

And were this world all devils o'er,
And watching to devour us,
We lay it not to heart so sore;
Not they can overpower us.
And let the prince of ill
Look grim as e'er he will,
He harms us not a whit:
For why? His doom is writ;
A word shall quickly slay him.

God's word, for all their craft and force
One moment will not linger,
But, spite of hell, shall have its course;
'Tis written by his finger.
And though they take our life,
Goods, honour, children, wife,
Yet is their profit small:
These things shall vanish all;
The city of God remaineth.

Translated by Thomas Carlyle

3   To Lewis Senfel at Munich, 4 October 1530

Grace and peace in Christ. Although my name is so hated that I must fear, my dear Lewis, that this letter will not be safely received and read by you, yet my love of music has overcome my fear, and in musical talent I see that God has richly endowed you. It is this that makes me hope my letter will bring no danger to you, for who even in Turkey would be offended at me for loving art and honouring an artist? Moreover I greatly honour and esteeym our two dukes of Bavaria, although they are not very favourable to me, because I see they love and foster music. I doubt not that there are many seeds of virtue in a mind touched by music, and I consider those not affected by it as stocks and stones. We know that music is hateful and intolerable to devils. I really believe, nor am I ashamed to assert, that next to theology there is no art equal to music, for it is the only one, except theology, which can give a quiet and happy mind, a manifest proof that the devil, the author of racking care and perturbation, flees from the sound of music as he does from the exhortation of religion. This is the reason why the prophets practised no other art, neither geometry nor arithmetic nor astronomy, as if they believed music and divinity nearly allied; as indeed they declare in their psalms and canticles. Praising music is like trying to paint a great subject on a small canvas, which turns out merely a daub. But my love for it abounds; it has often refreshed me and freed me from great troubles.

I pray you and beseech you if you have a copy of the canticle, I will lay me down in peace, to transcribe and send it to me. The tune delighted me even as a youth and does so more now that I know the words. I have never seen it arranged for several voices. I would not add to your labour, but if you have it so arranged I would be pleased. I hope my life is nearly at an end, for the world hates me and I am sick of it. I wish the good and faithful shepherd would take my soul. So I keep humming this canticle, and wishing I had it properly arranged. In case you do not know it I send along the air, which you can arrange after my death if you like. The Lord Jesus be with you always. Amen. Pardon my bold and tedious letter. Give my greetings to your whole choir.

COBURG
Smith, *Life and Letters*, 347 *et seq.*

4   Luther on Dancing

Dances are instituted that courtesy may be learned in company and friendship and acquaintance be contracted between young men and girls. Here their intercourse may be watched and occasion of honourable meeting given, so that having tried a girl we can afterwards let her go about more safely and easily. The Pope formerly condemned dances because he was an enemy of marriage. But let all things be done decently! Let honourable men and matrons be invited to see that everything is proper. I myself would attend them sometimes, but the youth would whirl less giddily if I did.

Smith, *Life and Letters*, 346 *et seq.*

5   Luther on Cicero

Cicero is the best philosopher, for he felt that the soul is immortal. He wrote best on natural, moral and rational philosophy. He is a valuable man, reading with judgement and able to express himself well. He wrote in earnest and did not fool like the Greeks Plato and Aristotle. I hope God will forgive such men as Cicero their sins. Even if he should not be redeemed, he will enjoy a situation in hell several degrees higher than that destined for our cardinal of Mainz.

Smith, *Life and Letters*, 342 *et seq.*

R   THE AUGSBURG CONFESSION

As an outlaw and a proscribed heretic, Luther was not able to attend the fateful Imperial Diet at Augsburg in 1530. He had instead to fidget in the castle of the Coburg, anxiously leaving the political fate of Protestantism to Philip Melanchthon. Melanchthon in fact acquitted himself nobly and presented a Protestant confession of faith which was to become a normative document of Lutheranism. At this juncture Melanchthon was prepared to disown the Protestant left wing, for the sake of better relations and more tolerance from the Catholic authorities.

I   The Augsburg Confession, 1530

The Confession is in two parts. Part I consists of twenty-one 'main articles of faith' and a summary; part II picks out seven 'articles in which [Catholic] abuses are corrected'.

PART I

1   GOD. [An orthodox Christian confession concerning the Trinity and the Father, condemning the classical heresies of the early centuries along with the Mohammedans.]

2   ORIGINAL SIN. Since the fall of Adam all men are, by the natural process of generation, born with sin, that is, without the fear of God, with no confidence [*fiducia*] towards God, and with concupiscence. This disease or flaw of origin is truly sin, condemning and bringing even now eternal death on those who are not reborn through baptism and the Holy Spirit.

Our Churches condemn the Pelagians and others who deny that the flaw in our origin is sin, and contend that man can be justified before God [*coram Deo*] by his own powers of reason, thus prejudicing the glory of the merit and blessings of Christ.

3   THE SON OF GOD. [Reaffirms the Christology of the Apostles' Creed.]

4   JUSTIFICATION. Men cannot be justified before God [*coram Deo*] by their own strength, merits or works, but are justified freely [*gratis*] through Christ by faith, when they believe that they are received into grace and their sins forgiven through Christ, who made satisfaction by his death for our sins. This faith God imputes for righteousness before Him [*coram ipso*]. *Romans* III and IV.

5   THE CHURCH'S MINISTRY. The Ministry of teaching the Gospel and offering the Sacraments is instituted that we may grasp this faith. For the Holy Spirit is given through the Word and the Sacraments, as it were through its instruments; and the Spirit creates faith, where and when God sees fit, in those who hear the Gospel; and this is be-

cause God justifies – not through our merits but through Christ – those who believe that they are received through Christ into grace.

Our Churches condemn the Anabaptists and those who think that the Holy Spirit comes to men without an outward word, merely by their own preparations and works.

6   THE NEW OBEDIENCE. [Good works, which God commands of us, are the *issue* of faith, not the means of earning justification.]

7   THE CHURCH. One holy Church will abide for ever. For the Church is the congregation of the saints, in which the Gospel is rightly taught and the sacraments are rightly administered. For the true unity of the Church it suffices to agree together concerning the teaching of the Gospel and the administration of the Sacraments; it is not necessary that everywhere should exist similar traditions of men, or similar rites and ceremonies instituted by men.

8   THE NATURE OF THE CHURCH. Although the Church is, properly speaking, the congregation of the saints and true believers, nevertheless, since many hypocrites and evildoers are mingled with them in this life, it is permissible to use the Sacraments which are administered by bad men . . . ; and the Sacraments and the Word take their efficacy from the ordaining and the mandate of Christ, even if they are shown forth by bad men.

Our Churches condemn the Donatists and others, who would deny that such ministry of bad men may be made use of in the Church. . . .

9   BAPTISM. Baptism is necessary to salvation; through it is offered the grace of God; children should be baptized, so that, offered through baptism to God, they may be received into his grace.

Our Churches condemn the Anabaptists, who reject the baptism of children and affirm that they can be saved without baptism.

10   THE LORD'S SUPPER. The body and blood of Christ are really present [*vere adsint*] and are distributed in the Lord's Supper to those who eat; our Churches reject those who teach otherwise.

11   CONFESSION. [The practice of private absolution should be retained.]

12   PENITENCE. [Absolution for post-baptismal sin must be always available in the church for the penitent. Penitence embraces *contrition* and *faith*; and good works, the fruit of penitence, must follow.] Our

Churches condemn the Anabaptists, who deny that the once-justified can ever lose the Holy Spirit, and insist that to some there comes so great perfection in this life that they cannot sin again. [Likewise the Novatians who refused to absolve the penitent, and others who bid us earn grace through satisfaction achieved by ourselves.]

13   THE USE OF THE SACRAMENTS. [Sacraments are 'signs and testimonies of the Will of God towards us'. The (Roman) *ex opere operato* is condemned, as ignoring faith.]

14   THE CHURCH'S ORDERS. None may publicly teach in church or administer the Sacraments who is not duly called [*rite vocatus*].

15   ECCLESIASTICAL RITES. [Rites which promote the Church's peace and good order may be observed, for example, holy days; but no such rite is necessary to salvation, and rites such as vows and fasting which claim to be meritorious for appeasing God are useless and contradict the Gospel.]

16   CIVIL AFFAIRS. [A Christian may properly be a magistrate, a judge, a soldier, hold property, swear oaths, marry.] Our Churches condemn the Anabaptists, who forbid these civil offices to Christians. [The state is an ordinance of God, and in all public relations love must be exercised.]

17   CHRIST'S RETURN TO JUDGEMENT. [Christ will return at the consummation to judge – the elect to eternal bliss, the wicked to eterna tormnt]. Our Churches condemn the Anabaptists, who limit thel duration of punishment for the wicked.

18   FREE WILL. The human will has a certain freedom for the securing of civil justice and the choosing of things that are subject to reason. But without the Holy Spirit it has not the power to secure the righteousness of God or spiritual righteousness. . . . For although nature can after a fashion achieve external actions (it can, for example, restrain a man from theft or murder), it cannot achieve inward motions (the fear of God, confidence towards him, chastity, patience etc.).

19   THE CAUSE OF SIN. [This is the will of the devil and of the ungodly, which voluntarily and in God's despite turns away from him.]

20   FAITH AND GOOD WORKS. [Re-statement of the essential Lutheran teaching.]

21   THE CULT OF THE SAINTS. [The saints are our examples, but not to be invoked or to be thought to help us in the way only Christ can – as mediator, reconciler, priest, intercessor.]

22   Such are the main heads of our teaching, and in it nothing can be found differing from scripture, or from the Catholic Church, or from the Church of Rome as we understand it from its [classical] writers. We are not heretics. Our trouble is with certain abuses which have crept into the Churches without any clear authority. . . . The ancient rites are to a large extent carefully preserved among us.

PART II

[The seven articles in which (Catholic) abuses are corrected concern – Communion in both kinds; the marriage of priests; the Mass; confession; fasts etc; monastic vows; the power of the Church.]

Latin in Kidd, Doc. 116*

2   To Melanchthon, 22 April 1530

Grace and peace in Christ! We have at last reached our Sinai, my dear Herr Philip, but out of this Sinai we shall make a Zion and build three tabernacles: one to the Psalter, one to the Prophets, and one to Æsop. But time is needed for this. This is a most agreeable spot, most suitable for study, only I miss you greatly.

I get quite excited when I think of the Turks and Mahomed, and of the diabolic fury which they vent on our bodies and souls. But at such times I shall pray fervently till he who dwells in heaven shall hear my petition. I see you are much distressed at the sight of those cowled monks who seem quite at home. But it is our fate to be spectators of the fierce onslaughts of these two realms and remain steadfast; and this onslaught is a sign and harbinger of our redemption. I pray that you may have refreshing sleep, and keep your soul free from care and from the fiery darts of the Evil One. Amen. I write this to while away my idle time, as my box with papers, etc., has not arrived. I have not seen the castle steward yet.

Meanwhile I want for nothing necessary to a solitary being. The great building which projects from the castle has been placed entirely at my disposal, and the keys of all the rooms have been put into my hands. There are over thirty men in the castle, among whom are twelve watchmen and two warders for the towers. But why write all this? only I have nothing else to write. Greet Dr Caspar Cruciger and Magister Spalatin from me. I shall greet Eisleben and Adler through Dr Jonas. From the region of the birds.

MARTIN LUTHER
Currie, 208 *et seq.*

3   To His Wife and Household, 28 April 1530

Grace and peace, my dear Kate, sirs, and friends! I have received all your letters telling me how you get along. I must now inform you that I, Magister Veit and Cyriac are not to be at the Diet, although we have one here. For there is a thicket just under our window like a small forest, where the daws and crows hold their diet, and such a running to and fro, and screaming night and day, that I often wonder they are not hoarse.

As yet I have not seen their emperor, but the courtiers are always prancing about dressed simply in black, with grey eyes, and all sing the same melody. They pay no heed to castle or hall; for their salon is vaulted by the beautiful canopy of heaven, while their feet rest on the broad fields with their green carpet and trees, the walls of their house reaching to the ends of the earth. They are independent of horses and carriages, for they have feathered wheels by which they escape the sportsmen's bullets. I fancy they have come together to have a mighty onslaught on corn, barley, wheat, etc. Many a knight will win his laurels here.

So here we sit, watching the gay life of song led by princes, etc., preparatory to a vigorous attack on the grain.

I always fancy it is the sophists and Papists I see before me, so that I may hear their lovely voices and their sermons, and see for myself what a useful kind of people these are who consume all the fruits of the earth, and then strut about in their grand clothing to while away the time.

Today we heard the first nightingale. The weather has been splendid. I commit you to God; see well to the house. . . .

MARTIN LUTHER
Currie, 209 *et seq.*

4   To Dr Gregory Brück at Augsburg, 5 August 1530

. . . I have recently seen two miracles. The first was, that as I looked out of my window, I saw the stars and the sky and the whole vault of

F

heaven, with no pillars to support it, and yet the sky did not fall and the vault reamined fast. But there are some who want to see the pillars and would like to clasp and feel them. And when they are unable to do so they fidget and tremble as if the sky would certainly fall in, simply because they cannot feel and see the pillars under it. If they could only do this, they would be satisfied that the sky would remain fast.

Again I saw great, thick clouds roll above us, so heavy that they looked like great seas, and I saw no ground on which they could rest nor any barrels to hold them and yet they fell not on us, but threatened us and floated on. When they had passed by, the rainbow shone forth, the rainbow which was the floor that held them up. It is such a weak thin little floor and roof that it was almost lost in the clouds and looked more like a ray coming through a stained-glass window than like a strong floor, so that it was as marvellous as the weight of the clouds. For it actually happened that this seemingly frail shadow held up the weight of water and protected us. But some people look at the thickness of the clouds and the thinness of the ray and they fear and worry. They would like to feel how strong the rainbow is, and when they cannot do so they think the clouds will bring on another deluge.

I permit myself such pleasantries with your honour, although I write with earnest purpose. . . . I hope we can keep the peace politically, but God's thoughts are above our thoughts. . . . If he should hear our prayers now and grant us peace, perhaps it would turn out worse than we hoped, and God would get less glory than the emperor. . . . I do not mean to despise the Emperor, and only hope and pray that he may do nothing against God and the imperial constitution. If, however, he does this, we as faithful subjects are bound to believe that it is not the emperor himself who is so doing, but tyrannical advisers usurping his authority, and we should make a distinction between the acts of our sovereign and those of his wicked counsellors. . . .

THE WILDERNESS   MARTIN LUTHER
                              Smith, *Life and Letters*, 259 et seq.

5   To Jerome Weller, Summer 1530

Whenever this temptation comes to you beware not to dispute with the devil nor allow yourself to dwell on these lethal thoughts, for so doing is nothing less than giving place to the devil and so falling. Try as hard as you can to despise these thoughts sent by Satan. In this sort of temptation and battle contempt is the easiest road to victory; laugh your enemy to scorn. . . .

We are conquered if we try too conscientiously not to sin at all. So when the devil says to you: 'Don't drink', answer him: 'I will drink, and right freely, just because you tell me not to.' One must always do what Satan forbids. What other cause do you think that I have for drinking so much strong drink, talking so freely and making merry so often, except that I wish to mock and harass the devil who is wont to mock and harass me. Would that I could contrive some great sin to spite the devil, that he might understand that I would not even then acknowledge it and that I was conscious of no sin whatever. We, whom the devil thus seeks to annoy, should remove the whole decalogue from our hearts and minds.

FESTE COBURG

Smith, *Life and Letters*, 324 *et seq*.

6   A Sermon on Keeping Children at School, 1530

Therefore I hope that the citizens will acknowledge the fidelity and the love of their lords by keeping their children in school and honestly helping to support this work, because they see that, without cost to themselves, their children are so rightly and diligently cared for and that everything is provided for them.

This mistake the preachers can easily provide against, for every community, and especially so great a city, must have more people in it than merchants, and other people who can do more than keep accounts and read German books. German books are made especially for the common man to read at home. But for preaching and governing and sitting in judgement, all the knowledge and all the languages in the world are too little of Germany only. This is particularly true in these days of ours, when one has to talk with other peoples more than with Neighbour Hans. . . .

By what I have said I do not want to insist that every man must train his child for this office, for not all the boys must become pastors, preachers and school-masters. It is well to know that the children of lords and great men are not to be used for this work, for the world needs heirs and people, otherwise the government will go to pieces. I am speaking of the common people, who used to have their children educated for the sake of the livings and benefices, and now keep them away, only for the sake of support. They do not need heirs, and yet they keep their children out of school, regardless of the fact that the children are clever and apt for these offices, and could serve God in them, without privation or hindrance. Such boys of ability ought to be kept at study, especially if they are poor men's sons, for all the foundations and monasteries and livings endowments were established for this purpose. Besides them, indeed, other boys ought also to study, even though they are not so clever, and ought to learn to understand, write and read Latin; for it is not only highly learned doctors and masters of holy scripture that we need. We must also have ordinary pastors, who will teach the Gospel and the Catechism to the young and the ignorant, and baptize and administer the Sacrament. They are of no use in a conflict with heretics, but that does not matter; in a good building we must have not only hewn facings, but also backing-stone; so we must have sacristans and other persons, who serve and help the preachers and the Word of God. . . .

Nevertheless government is a glorious ordinance of God and splendid gift of God, who has established and instituted it, and will have it maintained, as something that men cannot do without. If there were no worldly government, no man could live because of other men; one would devour the other, as the brute beasts do. Therefore as it is the function and the honour of the office of preaching to make sinners saints, and dead men live, and damned men saved, and the devil's children God's children; so it is the function and the honour of worldly government to make men out of wild beasts and to prevent men from becoming wild beasts. It keeps a man's body, so that not everyone may slay it; it keeps a man's wife, so that not everyone may seize and defile her; it keeps a man's child, his daughter or son, so that not everyone may carry them away and steal them; it keeps a man's house, so that not everyone may break in and commit outrage there; it keeps a man's fields and cattle and all his goods, so that not everyone may attack and steal and rob and damage them. There is nothing of this among the beasts, and if it were not for worldly government, there would be nothing of it among men, but they would cease to be men and become mere beasts. Do you think that, if the birds and beasts could speak, and were to see worldly government among men, they would say, 'O ye men! You are not men but gods, compared with us! How safe you live and hold your property, while among us no one is sure for an hour of life, or property, or means of livelihood, because of the others! Out upon your thanklessness, who do not see what a glorious life the God of all of us has given you compared with us beasts'? . . .

But I hold that it is the duty of the government to compel its subjects to keep their children in school, especially those children who were mentioned above. For it is truly its duty to maintain the offices and classes that have been mentioned, so that preachers, jurists, pastors, writers, physicians, schoolmasters and the like may continue, for we cannot do without them.

Philad. Edn., IV, 136 *et seq.*

7 To Hans Luther at Wittenberg, 19 June 1530

Grace and peace in Christ, dear little son. I am glad to hear that you are studying and saying your prayers. Continue to do so, my son, and when I come home I will bring you a pretty present.

I know a lovely, pleasant garden where many children are; they wear golden jackets and gather nice apples under the trees and pears cherries and purple plums and yellow plums, and sing and run and jump and are happy and have pretty little ponies with golden reins and silver saddles. I asked the man who owned the garden whose children they were. He said: 'They are the children who say their prayers and study and are good.' Then said I: 'Dear man, I also have a son whose name is Hans Luther; may he come into the garden and eat the sweet apples and pears and ride a fine pony and play with these children?' Then the man said: 'If he says his prayers and is good, he can come into the garden and Phil and Justy too, and when they all come they shall have whistles and drums and fifes and dance and shoot little cross-bows.' Then he showed me a fine large lawn in the garden for dancing, where hang real golden whistles and fine silver cross-bows. But it was yet early and the children had not finished eating and I could not wait to see them dance, so I said to the man: 'My dear sir, I must go away and write at once to my dear little Hans about all this, so that he will say his prayers and study and be good, so that he may come into the garden and he has an Auntie Lena whom he must bring with him.' So, dear little Hans, study and say your prayers and tell Phil and Justy to say their prayers and study too, so you may all come into the garden together. God bless you. Give Auntie Lena my love and a kiss from me.

Your loving father, MARTIN LUTHER

FESTE COBURG

Smith, *Life and Letters*, 351 *et seq.*

8   To Caspar Müller at Mansfeld, 19 January 1536

... Of the English embassy, as you at Mansfeld are so curious, I know
nothing especial. Queen Catherine has just died, and they say her
daughter is mortally ill. She lost her cause with all the world except
with us poor beggars the Wittenberg theologians. We would have kept
her in her royal honour as was right. But this is the end and final decision. The Pope acted in this matter like the Pope, promulgating con-
tradictory bulls and playing such a double game that it served him
right to be turned out of England, even if the evangelic teaching did
not profit thereby. He cheated the King so that I could almost excuse
his Majesty, though I do not approve all his acts. Friend, let us pray that
the Pope get a stroke of epilepsy. ...

WITTENBERG   DR MARTIN LUTHER
                                                    Smith, *Life and Letters*, 328

S   HISTORICAL BACKGROUND

The Emperor Charles V was a devout and loyal Catholic. At the Diet of Worms he said of Luther 'This man will never make me a heretic!' But he also learned, in following years, the need to wait and to compromise. For one thing, the manifold cares of his great dominions prevented him bringing any direct military pressure upon Thuringia, at the remote side of his empire. The menace of the Turks was a recurring spiral of anxiety; the 'great game' between the Pope and the King of France and himself was a long 'cold war' broken by bloody campaigns; there were troubles in Spain and Holland. Charles came to listen to moderate advice, and himself to distinguish perhaps between essentials and non-essentials of the faith. Hence the success of Protestant protests at the Diet of Speyer (1529) and Augsburg (1530) and the truce of 1532 which gave Luther and his friends a breathing space. The last ten years of Luther's life, however, saw a steady growth in Papal and Imperial power. The long-awaited Papal Council was not to meet until 1545, but in the last months of Luther's life the Emperor was able to lay military plans which a few months after Luther's death were to enable the imperial troops to overrun Thuringia and Saxony, and to take prisoner the two great Protestant princes, Philip of Hesse and John Frederick of Saxony. Something of the wrathful vehemence of Luther's last writings derives from this worsening situation.

1   Luther's Second Will, 6 January 1542

I, Martin Luther, recognize with my own hand, that I have given to my dear and faithful wife Kate, as her portion, or whatever it may be called, for her life, and to use at her pleasure and to her profit, and that I give her by this letter now and today, the following:

The property of Zulsdorf, as I bought it with the improvements, and all things as I have had it hitherto.

Item, Bruno's house, which I bought in the name of my servant Wolfgang Sieberger for him to dwell in.

Item, cups, jewels, rings, chains and gift-coins, which should be worth about a thousand gulden.

I do this,

First, because she has always been dear, worthy and fair, as my pious, true wedded wife, and has, by God's blessing, borne and brought up five children yet living (may God grant them long life).

Secondly, that she may meet the debt with which I am encumbered unless I do it during my lifetime, and pay it; as far as known it amounts to about four hundred and fifty gulden, but may well be more.

Thirdly and chiefly, because I want her not to look to the children but the children to her, to hold her in honour and submit to her as God has commanded. . . . Moreover I think a mother is the best guardian for her children, who will not use her property and portion to their injury and blood and she has carried them under her heart. . . .

Finally, I beg every one, that as in this bequest I do not use legal forms and words (for which I have good cause) they will recognize me to be what I am in truth, and am publicly known to be in heaven, on earth, and in hell, namely, one who has sufficient power and authority and who may be trusted and believed more than a notary. . . .

M.L.

Witnessed by Melanchthon, Cruciger and Bugenhagen

Smith, Life and Letters, 370 et seq.

T   LUTHER'S ILLNESSES

Luther's bodily ailments multiplied, and he suffered many things from many physicians. There was without doubt a connection between his spiritual anguishes (his *Anfechtungen*), which recurred throughout his life, and the palpitations and fainting fits which often accompanied them. Constipation and piles were excruciating annoyances on the Wartburg, but belong to this period of sedentary isolation. Bladder troubles and the stone culminated for him in the illness at Schmalkald, 1537, when he thought he would die. His eyesight and his hearing began to go in the 1540s. His death was from some kind of coronary seizure, whether cerebral or of the heart cannot at this date be determined.

I   To Justus Jonas at Wittenberg, 14 February 1537

Grace and peace in Christ. I wrote to you yesterday, dear Jonas, that is, on St. Valentine's eve; now I write you on the saint's day, as he keeps me here against my will. Last night Valentine began to make me convalescent from the stone; not indeed that Valentine who is the idol of epileptics, but the true and only valiant Valentine who saves those that trust in him. I hope that I shall at length be well by his grace. This is the eighth day since I stick or rather hang here, sick and tired of the place and of the inn and desirous of returning. For I am useless here. The princes and estates act differently from what I advised regardless of me. . . .

I am a beggar here, eating the bread of the Langrave of Hesse and the Duke of Württemberg (for they have the best loaves and fishes) and drinking of the wine of Nuremberg; our own Elector sends me meat and fish. You told me heavy bread caused the stone and now I learn it by experience, for that is the kind of bread we get here. I have the very best trout, but they are cooked in the same way and with the same water as the other fish. Oh, it is a merry dish! . . . Our Elector cares for me in all things and orders everything to be supplied to me as carefully as possible, but his orders are interfered with by his toadies, moadies, noadies and loadies. I have nothing else to write. Farewell in the Lord and pray for me.

CHALCIS   Yours, MARTIN LUTHER
                                 Smith, *Life and Letters*, 308 *et seq.*

2   From the Note-book of Veit Dietrich, Luther's Former Amanuensis

Saturday, 24 February, when Melanchthon burst into tears on seeing Luther, the latter said: '. . . Have we received good at the hands of the Lord and shall we not also receive evil? As the Lord willed so it has happened; blessed by the name of the Lord. In times past I have often played a dangerous game with the Pope and with the devil, but the Lord marvellously saved and strengthened me; why should I not now bear with equanimity what the Lord inflicts? My death is as nothing compared with that of the Son of God; many great and holy men have died before me, whose companions I am not worthy to be, but if I wish to be with them I must also die. Therefore I pray God with good courage, for our Lord is the Lord of life and has us in his hand.

'How quickly I am changed by disease – *Quantum mutatus ab illo!* But lately I wandered through the woods in good health. O God, we are nothing! I should like to pray our Lord God – even to complain a little – that I might die in my Saxony; if that cannot be I am ready to die when and where he calls me, and I shall die the enemy of all the enemies of my Lord Jesus Christ. If I die under the ban of the Pope, the Pope will die under the ban of my Lord Christ.'

The next day . . . he said: 'Dear Father, take my soul in thy hand. . . . Let me die. If this pain lasts longer, I shall go mad and fail to recognize thy goodness. If it were not for my faith in Christ I would kill myself. The devil hates me and has his claws in me, but do thou, God, avenge me on mine adversary; let me die and pay thou the devil as he deserves.'

Long afterwards he said:

'Oh, how I wanted my wife and children at Schmalkalden! I thought I would never see them more. How sorrowful that separation made me! I believe that the natural love of husband for wife and parents for children is greatest in dying people. But now that I am well again by God's grace, I love my wife and children all the more. No one is so spiritual as not to feel natural inclination and love, for the union of man and wife is a great thing.'

Smith, Life and Letters, 309 et seq

3   To Melanchthon at Schmalkalden, 27 February 1537

Dearest Philip: Blessed be God the Father of our Lord Jesus Christ, the Father of mercies and of all consolation, who this night at two o'clock took pity on me and relieved my sufferings. . . . At last I was able to pass water. . . .

I am writing at once. Please tell the news to my dear and gracious lords and all others, for I know how gladly they helped me. Let it go with me as God wills; I am ready to live or die, now that I have escaped from the pit into our own Saxony, and have here obtained grace. . . . May God preserve you all and beat down Satan and all his monstrous Roman allies under your feet. Amen. . . .

TAMBACH   Yours, MARTIN LUTHER
Smith, Life and Letters, 311

4 To Katherine Luther at Wittenberg, 27 February 1537

... Yesterday I left Schmalkalden in the Elector's private carriage. The reason I left was that for three days I have been very unwell, unable to pass water the whole time. I could not rest not sleep at night nor keep anything on my stomach. In short I was dead and commended you and the children to God and to my gracious Elector, thinking that I would never see you more. My heart was moved for you, for I thought I was surely in the grave. But men have prayed hard to God and perhaps some have wept before him, so that he has healed me this night. Wherefore thank God and ask the children and Aunt Lena to do the same, for you almost lost me. The good Elector did everything in his power for me but in vain. Moreover your medicine did not help me. But God wrought a miracle on me this night, and will continue to do so at the prayers of pious people. ...

TAMBACH   MARTIN LUTHER
                              Smith, *Life and Letters*, 311 *et seq.*

5 To Justus Jonas at Brunswick, 8 April 1538

... We confess Christ in quietness and confidence, but sometimes without much strength. We are oppressed by business, especially Melanchthon and I, on account of your absence, and I am sick of it, for I am an old veteran who has served his time and would prefer to spend my days in the garden enjoying the senile pleasures of watching God's wonders in the blooming of the trees, flowers and grass, and in the mating of the birds. I should have merited this pleasure and leisure had I not deserved to be deprived of it on account of my past sins. ...

WITTENBERG   Yours, MARTIN LUTHER
                              Smith, *Life and Letters*, 329 *et seq.*

6 To Wolfgang Sieberger, Luther's weak-minded Servant (Complaint of the birds in the Wittenberg wood to Luther) (no date)

To our good and kind Dr Martin Luther, preacher in Wittenberg.
We thrushes, blackbirds, linnets, gold-finches, along with other well-

disposed birds who are spending the summer at Wittenberg, desire to let you know that we are told on good authority that your servant, Wolfgang Sieberger, out of the great hatred he bears to us, has bought some old rotten nets to set up a fowling-ground for finches, and not only for our dear friends and finches, but in order to deprive us of the liberty of flying in the air and picking up grains of corn, and also to make an attempt upon our lives, although we have not deserved such a punishment at his hands.

Thus we poor birds humbly beseech you to prevent him carrying out his intentions, or if that be impossible, compel him to scatter corn for us in the evening, and forbid him rising before eight in the morning to visit the fowling-ground, and by doing this we shall ever be grateful to you, as it will enable us to take the route through Wittenberg. But if he continue his wicked attacks upon our lives, then we shall pray God to restrain him, and supply him with frogs, locusts and snails instead of us, and visit him with mice, lice, fleas and bugs in the nights, so that nothing may interfere with our freedom of flight.

Why does he not vent his wrath on the sparrows, magpies, crows, mice and rats which inflict so much injury on man, stealing the corn from the barns, which we never do, for we only pick up little fragments and single grains of corn, which we requite a hundredfold by swallowing flies, gnats and other insects?

We put our case before you in a common-sense way, to see if we are not cruelly treated in having so many snares laid for us.

But we trust God will allow us to escape from his foul rotten nets this autumn. Given in our celestial retreat among the trees under our common seal and signature.

'Behold the fowls of the air: for they sow not, neither do they reap, nor gather into barns; yet your heavenly Father feedeth them. Are ye not much better than they?'

Currie, 300 *et seq.*

7   Luther's Trousers

In 1539 Lauterbach heard Kate complain that her husband had cut a piece out of his son's trousers to supply his own. He defended himself thus:

The hole was so large that I had to have a large patch for it. Trousers seldom fit me well, so I have to make them last long. If the Electors Frederick and John had not better tailors than I have they would mend their own breeches. The Italian tailors are the best. They divide the labour, some making coats, some cloaks and some trousers. But in Germany they do it hit or miss, making all trousers according to one pattern. We praise the good old times but we live in the present. Think what an eye-sore it is to see a man with trousers like a pigeon and a coat so short that one can see his back between it and the trousers. There is a proverb that 'short-coated Saxons jump like magpies'.

Smith, *Life and Letters*, 316 *et seq.*

8   To Jerome Weller at Freiburg, 8 September 1540

Grace and peace. Dear Jerome, have nothing to do with those who wish to re-introduce houses of ill-fame. It would have been better never to have expelled the devil than to have done so only to bring him back again stronger than ever. Let those who favour this course deny the name of Christ and become as heathen ignorant of God. We who are Christians cannot do so. We have the plain text: 'Whoremongers and adulterers God will judge'; much more, therefore, will he judge those who protect and encourage vice. How can the priests preach against impurity if the magistrates encourage it? They allege the precedent of Nuremberg, but forget that she is the only town that has thus sinned. If the young men cannot contain, let them marry – indeed, what is the use of marriage if we permit vice unpunished? We have learned by experience that regulated vice does not prevent adultery and worse sins, but rather encourages them and condones them. . . . Let the magistrate punish one as well as the other, and if there is then secret vice, at least he is not to blame for it. We can neither do nor permit nor tolerate anything against God's command. We must do right if the world comes to an end. Farewell in haste.

WITTENBERG   DR MARTIN LUTHER
                                        Smith, *Life and Letters*, 321

9   To Katherine Jonas at Halle, 26 March 1542

Grace and peace. Kind, dear Friend! I humbly beg you to admonish your husband not to write so many promissory letters, for I don't like them and will excuse his promises for the future. His letters only say: 'I will write soon, I will write more, I will write something wonderful'; if he can write nothing but that, or what I know already, let him omit it.

Everything is going well here except that the treasury and taxation has run wild. Otherwise, living is so cheap as never before, a sack of corn for three groats. God bless you and yours. My Kate, now Lord of Zulsdorf, greets you kindly. She lets herself be rated at nine thousand gulden, including the Black Cloister, although she will not have an annual income of one hundred gulden from the property after my death. But my gracious lord has kindly given more than I asked. God bless you. Amen.

WITTENBERG   DR MARTIN LUTHER

Smith, *Life and Letters*, 371 *et seq.*

10   The Death of Magdalene Luther, September 1542

As his daughter lay very ill, Dr Luther said: 'I love her very much, but dear God, if it be thy will to take her, I submit to thee.' Then he said to her as she lay in bed: 'Magdalene, my dear little daughter, would you like to stay here with your father, or would you willingly go to your Father yonder?' She answered: 'Darling father, as God wills'. Then said he: 'Dearest child, the spirit is willing but the flesh is weak.' Then he turned away and said: 'I love her very much; if my flesh is so strong, what can my spirit do? God has given no bishop so great a gift in a thousand years as he has given me in her. I am angry with myself that I cannot rejoice in heart and be thankful as I ought.'

Now as Magdalene lay in the agony of death, her father fell down before the bed on his knees and wept bitterly and prayed that God might free her. Then she departed and fell asleep in her father's arms. . . .

As they laid her in the coffin he said: 'Darling Lena, you will rise and shine like a star, yea, like the sun. . . . I am happy in spirit, but the flesh is sorrowful and will not be content, the parting grieves me beyond measure. . . . I have sent a saint to heaven.'

Smith, *Life and Letters*, 353 *et seq.*

U   THE BIGAMY OF PHILIP OF HESSE

The bigamy of Philip of Hesse in 1541 brought disrepute upon himself and on the Reformers who connived at it. His liaison with Margaret von der Saal was complicated for him by the fact that her mother demanded that Philip marry her daughter. To his credit he had not taken her as a mistress, but his conscience prevented him from attending the Sacrament. The Reformer Martin Bucer, who was closest to him, suggested as a way out that a dispensation be given him *in foro conscientiae* by which he might secretly marry Margaret without divorcing his legal wife. It was of the essence of this that it be kept secret, and Melanchthon and Luther reluctantly gave their consent to this way out. Margaret's mother would have none of the secrecy and it was obvious that an open scandal must result. Melanchthon had a nervous collapse: Luther on the other hand went into a towering rage and threatened to denounce the whole business. It was a sorry example of the Reformers themselves using a dubious device borrowed from the medieval Church, that of a dispensation, though medieval canon law would not have allowed a dispensation for bigamy.

I   To Philip, Landgrave of Hesse, at Schmalkalden, 10 April 1540

Grace and peace. Most serene, noble Prince, gracious Lord! I have received your Grace's letter and note that you are pleased with our counsel, which we would willingly have kept secret. Melanchthon has written me nothing about your Grace, but will certainly do so, or tell me about it orally. But we want to keep the business a secret for the sake of the example, which every one would follow, even at last the coarse peasants. There are also other reasons as great or even greater why you should keep it to yourself and not avow it which would make us a lot of trouble. Wherefore your Grace will please be secret and improve your life as you promised. Our dear Lord be with your Grace. Amen.

Your Grace's obedient servant, MARTIN LUTHER
Smith, *Life and Letters*, 375

2   To Antony Lauterbach at Pirna, 2 June 1540

Grace and peace. In answer to your question about the Landgrave's second marriage, dear Antony, I can say nothing. I have only heard that the girl Von der Saal has given birth to a boy,[1] but I know not whether it was true. If it is true and he recognizes that he is the father and supports the mother and child, it seems that he will do right. Per-

---

[1] The rumour was false.

haps this is the cause of the rumour. I only know that no public proofs of the marriage have been shown me. There are heirs from the legitimate wife who will not permit – nor will the princes – that the children of another wife should become co-heirs, especially if the second wife be of inferior rank. Therefore let those rail who wish to do so until time show what the monster really is. One must not pronounce rashly on insufficient evidence about the doings of princes. I will instruct your assistant about the other things.

WITTENBERG

MARTIN LUTHER
Smith, *Life and Letters*, 376

3   To John Frederick, Elector of Saxony, 10 June 1540

Most serene, highborn Elector, most gracious Lord! I am sorry to learn that your Grace is importuned by the court of Dresden about the Landgrave's business. Your Grace asks what answer to give the men of Meissen. As the affair was one of the confessional, both Melanchthon and I were unwilling to communicate it even to your Grace, for it is right to keep confessional matters secret, both the sin confessed and the counsel given, and had the Landgrave not revealed the matter and the confessional counsel, there would never need have been all this nauseating unpleasantness.

I still say that if the matter was brought before me today, I should not be able to give counsel different from what I did. Setting apart the fact that I know I am not as wise as they think they are, I need conceal nothing, especially as it has already been made known. The state of affairs is as follows: Martin Bucer brought a letter and pointed out that, on account of certain faults in the Landgrave's wife the Landgrave was not able to keep himself chaste and that he had hitherto lived in a way which was not good, but that he would like to be at one with the principal heads of the Evangelic Church, and he declared solemnly before God and his conscience that he could not in future avoid such vices unless he were permitted to take another wife. We were deeply horrified at this tale and at the offence which must follow, and we begged his Grace not to do as he proposed, but we were told again that he could not abandon his project, and if he could not obtain what he wanted from us, he would disregard us and turn to the Emperor and Pope. To prevent this we humbly begged that if his Grace would not, or, as he averred before God and his conscience, could not do otherwise, yet that he could keep it a secret. Though necessity compelled him, yet he could not defend his act before the world and the imperial laws; this he promised to do and we accordingly agreed to help him before God and cover it up as much as possible with such examples as that of Abraham. This all happened as though in the confessional, and no one can accuse us of having acted as we did willingly or voluntarily or with pleasure or joy. It was hard enough for our hearts, but we could not prevent it; we thought to give his conscience such counsel as we could.

I have indeed learned several confessional secrets, both while I was still a Papist and later, which, if they were revealed, I should have to deny or else publish the whole confession. Such things belong not to the secular courts nor are they to be published. God has here his own judgement and must counsel souls in matters where no worldly law nor wisdom can help. My preceptor in the cloister, a fine old man, had many such affairs, and once had to say of them, with a sigh: 'Alas, alas, such things are so perplexed and desperate that no wisdom, law, nor reason can avail; one must commend them to divine goodness.' So instructed, I have accordingly in this case also acted agreeably to divine goodness.

But had I known that the Landgrave had long satisfied his desires, and could well satisfy them with others, as I have now just learned that he did with her of Eschwege, truly no angel would have induced me to give such counsel: I gave it only in consideration of his unavoidable necessity and weakness, and to put his conscience out of peril, as Bucer represented the case to me. Much less would I ever have advised that there should be a public marriage, to which (though he told me nothing of this) a young princess and young countess should come, which is truly not to be borne and is insufferable to the whole empire. But I understood and hoped, as long as he had to go the common way with sin and shame and weakness of the flesh, that he would take some honourable maiden or other in secret marriage, even if the relation did not have a legal look before the world. My concession was on account of the great need of his conscience – such as has happened to other great lords. In like manner I advised certain priests in the Catholic lands of Duke George and the bishops secretly to marry their cooks.

This was my confessional counsel about which I would much rather have kept silence, but it has been wrung from me and I could do nothing but speak. But the men of Dresden speak as though I had taught the same for thirteen years, and yet they give us to understand what a friendly heart they have to us, and what great desire for love and unity, just as if there were no scandal nor sin in their lives which are ten times worse before God than anything I ever advised. But the world must always smugly rail at the mote in its neighbour's eye and forget the beam in its own eye. If I must defend all I have said or done in former years, especially at the beginning, I must beg the Pope to do the same, for if they defend their former acts (let alone their present ones) they would belong to the devil more than to God.

I am not ashamed of my counsel, even if it should be published in all the world, but for the sake of the unpleasantness which would then follow, I should prefer, if possible, to have it kept secret.

WITTENBERG   MARTIN LUTHER, *with his own hand*
                                    Smith, *Life and Letters*, 377 *et seq.*

V   LUTHER'S DOCTRINE OF THE CHURCH

Luther, against an over-institutionalized Church, returned to the thought of it as essentially a 'communion of saints' and a community of believers. Here are some of his aphorisms about it:

When I call the Church a spiritual assembly, you have insultingly taken me to mean I would build a church as Plato builds a state that never was. (*Against Emser*, 1521)

Thank God a child of seven knows what the Church is – the holy believers and the lambs who hear their shepherd's voice. (*Schmalkaldic articles*, 1537)

Oh, it is a high, deep, hidden thing is the Church which nobody may perceive or see, but only grasp by faith in baptism, Word and Sacrament. (*Against Hans Worst*, 1541)

The summoning of the Papal Council meant, necessarily, that Luther should think and write about the authority of the Church, and two treatises of his last decade – *Of Councils and the Church* (**V, 1**) and *Against the Papacy* (the last a virulent diatribe of small theological value) – expound his views on the subject.

I 'On the Councils and the Church', 1539

... Well then, the Children's Creed teaches us (as was said) that a Christian holy people is to be and to remain on earth until the end of the world. This is an article of faith that cannot be terminated until that which it believes comes, as Christ promises, 'I am with you always, to the close of the age' [*Matthew* XXVIII: 20]. But how will or how can a poor confused person tell where such Christian holy people are to be found in this world? Indeed, they are supposed to be in this life and on earth, for they of course believe that a heavenly nature and an eternal life are to come, but as yet they do not possess them. Therefore they must still be in this life and remain in this life and in this world until the end of the world. For they profess, 'I believe in another life'; thereby they confess that they have not yet arrived in the other life, but believe in it, hope for it, and love it as their true fatherland and life, while they must yet remain and tarry here in exile – as we sing in the hymn about the Holy Spirit, 'As homeward we journey from this exile. Lord, have mercy.' We shall now speak of this.

First, the holy Christian people are recognized by their possession of the holy Word of God.

Second, God's people or the Christian holy people are recognized by the Holy Sacrament of baptism, wherever it is taught, believed, and administered correctly according to Christ's ordinance. That too is a public sign and a precious, holy possession by which God's people are sanctified.

Third, God's people, or Christian holy people, are recognized by the holy Sacrament of the Altar, wherever it is rightly administered, believed, and received, according to Christ's institution.

Fourth, God's people or holy Christians are recognized by the office of the keys exercised publicly. That is, as Christ decrees in *Matthew* XVIII [:15-20], if a Christian sins, he should be bound in his sin and cast out. If he does mend his ways, he should be absolved. That is the office of the keys.

Fifth, the Church is recognized externally by the fact that it consecrates or calls ministers, or has offices that it is to administer.

Sixth, the holy Christian people are externally recognized by prayer, public praise, and thanksgiving to God. Where you see and hear the Lord's Prayer prayed and taught; or psalms or other spiritual songs sung, in accordance with the Word of God and the true faith; also the Creed, the Ten Commandments, and the Catechism used in public, you may rest assured that a holy Christian people of God are present.

Seventh, the holy Christian people are externally recognized by the holy possession of the sacred cross. They must endure every misfortune and persecution, all kinds of trials and evil from the devil, the world, and the flesh (as the Lord's Prayer indicates) by inward sadness, timidity, fear, outward poverty, contempt, illness, and weakness, in order to become like their head, Christ. . . .

First, nobody can deny that we, as well as the Papists, have received holy baptism and because of that are called Christians. . . .

Second, nobody will deny that we have the holy Sacrament of the Altar, just as Christ himself instituted it and the Apostles and the whole of Christendom have since practised it. . . .

Third, nobody can deny that we have the true and ancient keys, and do not use them in any other way than to bind and loose sins, committed against the command of God. . . .

Fourth, nobody can deny that we have in fulness and purity the preaching office and the Word of God. . . .

Fifth, nobody can deny that we, like it, do indeed hold, believe, sing, and confess the Apostles' Creed, the ancient Creed of the ancient Church, and neither make nor add anything new to it. . . .

Sixth, nobody can deny that we have the same prayer as the ancient Church, the same Lord's Prayer. . . .

Seventh, nobody can deny that with the ancient Church we hold and teach that no one should honour and not curse the temporal powers and should not compel them to kiss the Pope's feet.

Eighth, nobody can deny that we praise and honour marriage as a divine, blessed, and well-pleasing ordinance of God's creation for the procreation of children and prevention of carnal unchastity. . . .

Ninth, nobody can deny that we experience the same suffering (as St. Peter says [*I Peter* v:9]) as our brethren in the world. . . .

Tenth, nobody can deny that we have not shed blood, murdered, hanged or avenged ourselves in return, as we could often have done and could still do. . . .

This is the first, real, fundamental beginning of the Lutheran rumpus, which the bishop of Mainz, not Duke Frederick, began with that fleecer and pick-pocket, Tetzel. Indeed, it goes back rather to Tetzel's blasphemous preaching, which (as you have heard) was aimed at stealing and robbing the people of their money to pay for the bishop's pallium and pomp. Yet after having been admonished by me, he would not stop Tetzel, but rather increased the price and wanted to steal far more money than he had already stolen under the guise of Indulgences; thus he showed regard for neither the truth nor the salvation of men's souls. This shameless cleric, who knows all this perfectly well, now wants to lay the blame at the feet of a worthy prince who has since died [Frederick the Wise]. He shamelessly breathes and instills these lies into his Harrys. Now if a rumpus has come out of this, and discontent with these slanderous Harrys, these infamous Mainzes, these effeminate cowards, these desperate scoundrels and their whole hellish crew, they may thank the bishop of Mainz for it. He began it with his execrable thieving greed and his blasphemous Tetzel, whom he sent out and defended. And if Luther had not attacked Tetzel's blasphemous preaching, which at that time had gone so far and with such power, wood and stones would have cried out against it; not a gentle Lutheran rumpus, but an abominably devilish one would have been the result. If they were to tell the truth, they have been safe until now under our protection, that is, under God's word. Otherwise, the sects would indeed have taught them manners.

The other cause for the beginning of this rumpus was the most Holy Father, Pope Leo, with his untimely ban. Doctor Sow [John Eck] and all the Papists helped him with it, as did a number of silly asses, indeed, everyone who wanted to win his spurs at my expense. They wrote and ranted against me, that is, whoever could hold a pen in his hand. But I hoped the Pope would protect me because I had so secured and armed my disputation with scripture and Papal decretals that I was sure the Pope would damn Tetzel and bless me. I also dedicated the Explanations to him with a humble essay, and this book of mine greatly pleased even many cardinals and bishops. For I was at that time a better papist than Mainz and Harry have ever been, or could possibly be, and the Papal decretals say quite clearly that Indulgence sellers cannot redeem souls from purgatory with Indulgences. But while I waited for the blessing from Rome, thunder and lightning came. I had to be the sheep who troubled the water for the wolf. Tetzel went free, but I had to be eaten.

In addition, they treated me in such a fine popish way that I was, to be sure, damned in Rome sixteen days before the citation came to me.

Philad. Edn., V, 131 *et seq.*

2   To His Wife, Katherine, 6 February 1546

To the deeply learned lady, Katherine Luther, my gracious consort at Wittenberg, grace and peace! Dear Kate – We sit here in martyrdom,

longing to be away, but I fancy that cannot be for eight days. Ask M.
Philip to correct his exposition, for he does not seem to understand why
the Lord calls riches thorns. This is the school in which to learn that.
But it is disagreeable to me that the thorns should always be threatened
with fire in the scriptures; therefore I should be the more patient in
order, with God's help, to be able to achieve something good. Thy sons
are still at Mansfeld. We have enough to eat and drink, and would
otherwise have a very good time if this troublesome business were only
at an end. It seems as if the devil were mocking us, but God will requite
him with the same. Amen. Pray for us. The messenger is impatient.

MARTIN LUTHER
Currie, 147

3   To Katherine, 7 February 1546

To my dear wife, Katherine Luther, doctoress and self-tormentor at
Wittenberg, my gracious lady. Grace and peace in the Lord!

Do thou read, dear Kate, the Gospel of St. John and the little catechism of which you once said, 'This book tells all about me'? For thou
must needs assume the cares of thy God, as if he were not Almighty,
and could not create ten Dr Martins if the old one were suffocated in
the Saale or in the stove, or . . . Leave me in peace with thy cares! I
have a better protector than thou and all the angels. He it is who lay
in the manger and was fondled on a maiden's breast, but was at the
same time seated on the right hand of God, the Almighty Father. Therefore be at rest. Amen! I think that hell and the whole world must at
present be free from devils, who, perhaps because of me, have all now
gathered in Eisleben, to such a pass things seem to have come here. It
is said that at Ritzdorf, close to Eisleben, where the wind blew so
fiercely upon me, four hundred Jews walk and ride out and in. Count
Albrecht, who owns all the land round Eisleben, has refused his protection to the Jews. There are often as many as fifty in one house here,
as I wrote to you. Still no one will injure them. The Countess of Mansfeld, widow of Solms, is looked upon as their protector. I do not know
if all this be true, but I have given my opinion pretty freely on the subject today, whether it will help or not. Pray, pray, pray, and thus help
us to right matters. Today I felt inclined to mount my carriage and set
off, but my anxiety as to my Fatherland held me back. I have now become a lawyer (*jurist*), but that will lead to nothing. It would have been
better had they allowed me to remain a divine. If spared, I should like

to appear among them as a hobgoblin, so that I, through the grace of God, might set bounds to their pride. They try to pose as God, but they would be wise to retreat in time before their Godhead is changed into a devil, as happened to Lucifer, who could not remain in heaven on account of his pride. Well, well, the will of the Lord be done! Let M. Philip read this letter, for I have not time to write to him, so you may comfort yourself that I love you dearly, since, as you know, I always write when I can, and he will understand this, having a wife himself.

We live well here, and the Council sends me for every meal about a hogshead of good Rhine wine. Sometimes I drink it with my friends. The Naumburg beer is also very good. The devil has ruined all the beer in the land with pitch, which causes phlegm to accumulate in my breast, and with you has he destroyed the wine with brimstone. But here the wine is pure, except what is made in the district. And know all that the letters you have written have arrived, and today I have received those you wrote last Friday along with M. Philip's, so that you may not be angry. Your beloved lord,

MARTIN LUTHER
Currie, 471 *et seq.*

4   To Katherine, 10 February 1546

To the saintly, anxious lady, Katherine Luther, owner of Zulsdorf, at Wittenberg, my gracious dear wife. Grace and peace in Christ! Most saintly lady doctoress, we thank you kindly for your great care for us, which prevented you sleeping, for since you began to be so anxious we were nearly consumed by a fire in our inn just outside my room door; and yesterday, doubtless on account of your anxiety, a stone fell upon our heads and almost crushed us as in a mouse-trap; and over and above, in our own private room, lime and mortar came down for two days, and when the masons came – after only touching the stone with two fingers – it fell, and was as large as a large pillow, and two hand-breadths wide. We had to thank your anxious care for all this, but happily the dear, holy angels guarded us also. I fear if you do not cease being anxious the earth may at last swallow us up and the elements pursue us. Is it thus thou hast learnt the Catechism and the faith? Pray and leave it to God to care for us, as he has promised in the fifty-fifth Psalm and many other places, 'Cast thy burden on the Lord, and he shall sustain thee.' Thank God we are fresh and well, except that we are getting tired of the whole business, and nothing would satisfy Dr Jonas but to have a sore leg also, having knocked it against a chest; so great is the power of human envy, that he would not permit me to be the sole possessor of a lame leg. I herewith commit you to God. We would gladly be free and set out on our homeward journey, if God permitted it. Amen. Amen. Amen. Your obedient servant,

MARTIN LUTHER
Currie, 473 *et seq*

5   To Katherine, 14 February 1546

Luther's last letter to his wife is preserved in the room in which he died in Eisleben. He preached for the last time on *Matthew* XII: 25, exhorting the people to cleave to the Lord and Master, who calls the weak and weary to himself, 'I could say much more, but am weak, so will leave it alone,' he concluded. Luther died on 18 February.

To my dear kind wife, Katherine Luther, at Wittenberg. Grace and peace in the Lord! Dear Kate – We hope to return home this week, if God will. God has richly manifested his grace towards us here, for the lords through their Council, have arranged everything, except two or three things, one of which is that the two brothers, Counts Gebhardt and Albrecht, should again become brothers, which I shall try to accomplish today, through inviting them to be my guests – so that they may converse with one another, for till now they have been dumb, embittering each other with letters.

In other respects the young gentlemen have been very happy, riding out together on sledges with the tinkling of fools' bells, the young ladies accompanying them, all joking and in high spirits, Count Gebhardt's son being among the number.

From this one may see that God is the hearer of prayer.

I send you some trout, which the Countess Albrecht has sent me. She is delighted with the reconciliation. Your sons are still at Mansfeld. Jacob Luther will see well to them. We are provided with meat and drink like lords, and have every attention paid us – indeed too much, so that we might forget you at Wittenberg. I am very well.

But Dr Jonas's leg has been very bad, holes appearing in the skin, but God will help. You may show this to Magister Philip, Dr Pommer, and Dr Cruciger! It is reported here that Dr Martin has been snatched away by the devil. The report comes from Leipzig and Magdeburg. It is the invention of these wiseacres, your countrymen.

Some declare that the Emperor is thirty miles from here, at Soest in Westphalia; others that the French are enlisting recruits, and the Landgrave also.

But let us say and sing, that we shall wait and see what God will do. I commend you to God.

MARTIN LUTHER
Currie, 474 *et seq.*

6   Luther's 'Autobiographical Fragment', March 1545

Martin Luther greets his pious readers.

Long and hard have I resisted those who wished me to publish my books – or rather the disordered products of my sleepless nights. I had no wish for the works of the old writers to be eclipsed by my novelties or to impede the student from reading them. What is more, there are now available, by God's grace, very many systematic writings – and above all Philip [Melanchthon]'s *Loci Communes* – by which a theologian or a bishop can be given an abundance of attractive training to become proficient in preaching sound doctrine. Above all, Holy Writ can now be had in nearly every living language. My books, on the other hand, were prompted or rather dictated by the bewildering pressure of events, and consequently resemble the 'primitive and disordered chaos' [Ovid, *Metamorphoses* 1:7] so that even I can no longer sort them out with ease.

For these reasons I desired hitherto that all my books should be buried in perpetual oblivation, to make room for better ones. But I have been overcome by the shameless and untiring importunity of others, who daily deafened me with their warnings that if I did not allow publication during my life-time, editors would assuredly get to work after my death who would have no knowledge of the causes and contexts of the subject-matter, and so would make confusion far worse confounded. They were seconded by the wish – the command – of our illustrious Prince John Frederick, the Elector, who ordered and even compelled the printers not only to go to press but to bring out their edition in double-quick time.

My main concern, however, is to beg my pious reader, for the sake of our Lord Jesus Christ himself, to read my books judiciously – or rather with much mercy. He should realize that I was once a monk, and that when I first took up this cause [the attack on Indulgences] I was a most vehement Papist, so intoxicated – so drowned – in papal dogmas that I stood ready beyond all others to kill, if I could, or at least to consent to and work with the killers, of every one who depreciated even by a single syllable the obedience due to the Pope. I was just such a Saul as the many that exist today. I offered no such ice-cold defence of the Papacy as did Eck and his like, who seemed to me to defend the Pope for the purpose of filling their own stomachs rather than from serious conviction – indeed, they seem to me to this day really to be laughing at him, like so many Epicureans. I was in deadly earnest, as a man who had a dreadful fear of the Last Day and yet longed from the bottom of his heart for salvation.

This is why you will find in my earlier writings such a multitude of grovelling concessions to the Pope, which as time has proceeded I abominate and repudiate for extreme blasphemy. You will, then, pious reader, lay this error – or as my critics falsely describe it, this self-contradiction – to the charge of the time and my inexperience. In those early days I stood alone; I was fitted neither by experience nor education for dealing with such momentous subjects: and I call God to witness that I plunged into these controversies neither by choice nor conviction, but by chance.

When then, in 1517 Indulgences were being sold in these districts (or 'promulgated', as I preferred to call it) for filthy lucre, I, who was in those days a preacher – what is called a young Doctor of Theology – began to dissuade and deter the people from lending their ear to the cries of the Indulgence-mongers, for there were to hand means of much greater good; and I conceived that in this I could claim the Pope as my protector, for I placed strong reliance on his good faith when he condemned through his decrees in the clearest terms the avarice of these 'quaestors' (as he called the preachers of Indulgences).

I went on to write two letters; one was to Albert, Archbishop of Mainz (who was actually going halves on the proceeds of the Indulgences with the Pope – something I did not then know), and the other to our so-called Ordinary, Jerome the Bishop of Brandenburg, asking him to repress the impudence and blasphemy of the 'quaestors'. But I was only a poor little brother, and they despised me. Stung by this I published a list [of Theses] for disputation and at the same time in German a sermon on Indulgences, and a little later the Resolutions, in which my concern was to shield the Pope's honour by pressing not for the condemnation of Indulgences but for preference to be given to works of love.

This was indeed to rend the heavens and consume the world with fire! Accusation was laid against me to the Pope: I was cited to appear in Rome; the whole Papacy arose against me and me alone. All this happened in 1518, when Maximilian held the diet at Augsburg, and Cardinal Cajetan served as papal legate. The most illustrious Duke Frederick of Saxony, Elector and Prince, approached him on my behalf and secured me exemption from the summons to Rome, and instead a summons before the cardinal himself, who should investigate and decide the issue. Soon the diet came to an end.

Meanwhile the Germans had wearied of the plunderings, traffickings and boundless deceits of the rogues from Rome, and they were awaiting with bated breath the outcome of so great an issue, which no previous bishop or theologian had dared to touch. In any case public opinion was blowing in my favour, because everyone hated the Romish artifices with which they had filled and exhausted the whole earth.

And so I came to Augsburg, a poor traveller on foot, but armed with provisions and a letter of commendation from Prince Frederick to the Senate and to certain men of good-will. I was there three days before I went on to the cardinal, for those excellent friends held me back and urged me with all their power not to approach him without a safe-conduct from the emperor. Every day, however, the cardinal summoned me through a spokesman of his, who was a great nuisance with his insistence that if I would only revoke, all would be well. But my grievance was too long-standing to permit of an easy way out.

At last, on the third day, the spokesman came demanding to know why I kept away from the cardinal, who was awaiting me in the kindest spirit. I replied that I could not go against the advice of my excellent friends, to whom I had been commended by Prince Frederick, and who would not hear of my going to the cardinal without the emperor's protection or safe-conduct. Once I had it (which they were working for through the imperial senate) I would come at once. At this he lost patience. 'Do you imagine that Prince Frederick will take up arms on *your* behalf?' 'I certainly should not wish him to.' 'Then where will you stay?' 'Under the sky,' I replied. Then he said, 'If you had the Pope and the cardinals in your power, what would you do?' 'I would show them,' I answered, 'all reverence and honour.' Then he, with a derisive Italian gesture, said 'Hem!', and off he went and never came back.

On the same day the imperial senate informed the cardinal that the emperor's protection or safe-conduct had been granted me, and warned him against harbouring designs of too great severity against me. He is said to have replied, 'Very well. I shall however do my duty.'

Such were the beginnings of all that trouble. The rest you can learn from the account of the proceedings included below.

During that year Master Philip Melanchthon had already been summoned here by Prince Frederick to teach Greek literature, doubtless to give me a colleague in my theological work. His writings attest sufficiently what the Lord has accomplished through this instrument of His, not just in literature but in theology, let the devil and his agents rage as they will.

In the following year, 1519, Maximilian died in February, and by the law of the empire Duke Frederick took his place. This led to some easing of the stormy situation, and gradually there arose a contempt for excommunications and Papal thunderbolts. For when Eck and Caraccioli brought a Bull from Rome condemmning Luther, and each of the found opportunity to bring it to the notice of Duke Frederick, who was at Cologne at the time along with other princes in order to meet the recently elected Charles, Frederick was most indignant about it and with great courage and firmness rebuked that rascally Papalist, because along with Eck he had disturbed his own and his brother John's domains behind his back; he reproved Caraccioli with such majesty that the two men departed quite crestfallen and ashamed. The prince was blessed with incredible insight to see through the strategems of the Roman Curia and to deal with them as they deserved. He kept his nose very clean and could smell out more things from a greater distance than the Romanists could either hope or fear.

This is why, after that, they did not put him to the test again. Even on the so-called 'Golden Rose',[1] sent him that very year by Leo X, he put no value but rather ridiculed it; and so the Romanists were forced to give up in despair their attempts to deceive so great a prince. The Gospel spread and prospered under his protection, and was propagated far and wide. His authority influenced a great number; his supreme wisdom and keen-sightedness secured him from the suspicion (except among the ill-disposed) of wishing to nourish and protect heresy or heretics, and this did the Papacy great harm.

The same year the Disputation of Leipzig was held, when Eck challenged Carlstadt and myself, but I could not get a safe-conduct from Duke George although I wrote him repeatedly; so I came to Leipzig not as a debator but an observer, under the safe-conduct granted to Carlstadt. I do not know who had blocked my application, for hitherto Duke George (as I knew for certain) had been on my side.

---

[1] A kind of 'Nobel Prize' awarded annually by the Pope to an outstanding ruler. Frederick merely sent three representatives to Altenburg to receive it on his behalf.

Here Eck came to my lodging and said he had heard that I was refusing to debate. I replied, 'How can I debate, when I can't get a safe-conduct from Duke George?' He said, 'If I can't debate with you, I've no wish to debate with Carlstadt either, for I came here on your account. If I get you a safe-conduct, will you debate with me then?' 'Get it,' I said, 'and I will'. He left, and soon a safe-conduct, with full liberty of public debate, was granted me.

Eck did this because he foresaw a chance of distinguishing himself in dealing with my thesis that the Pope had no divine right to be head of the Church. Here a wide field lay open to him and a supreme opportunity of winning the favour of the Pope by flattery and applause, while at the same time overwhelming me with hatred and disgust. He followed this line vigorously throughout the debate, but he neither proved his own case nor refuted mine. Duke George himself said to the two of us at breakfast, 'Well, divine right or no, he's still the Pope.' He would never have said this if the arguments hadn't left their mark on him, but simply approved Eck's case alone.

Here, in my case, you should observe how hard it is to struggle clear of errors which have been confirmed by the example of the whole world, and which long habit has turned into second nature. How true is the proverb, 'It is hard to give up what one is used to',[1] and the other, 'Custom is second nature'.[2] How truly Augustine remarks, 'Custom, if it is not resisted, becomes necessity'.[3] I, who at that time had been reading and teaching the holy scriptures most diligently in private and in public for seven years, so that I knew them nearly all by heart, and who had by then acquired the firstfruits of knowledge and faith in Christ – that we become righteous and are saved not by works but by faith in Christ – and finally who was already defending in public the thesis of which I am speaking – that the Pope is not the head of the Church by divine right – even *I* did not then draw the conclusion that the Pope must needs be of the devil. For that which is not from God must necessarily be from the devil.

As I have said, I was so habituated to the example of holy Church and the title it used, as well as to my own customary language, that I conceded human right to the Pope, which however unless it rests on divine authority is a lie and from the devil. For we obey parents and magistrates not because they prescribe it but because such is the will of God (*I Peter* III [:2-13]). This is why I can tolerate with some equa-

[1] Juvenal, *Satires*, VI. 87.
[2] Cicero, *De Finibus*, V.25, 74.
[3] Augustine, *Confessions*, viii.5, 10.

nimity those who cling pertinaciously to the Papacy, especially those who have not read sacred or even profane writings, when I, who read the scriptures for so many years with such diligent care, could cling to it so tenaciously myself.

In 1519, Leo X, as I have said, sent the Rose by Karl von Miltitz, and he urged me repeatedly to be reconciled with the Pope. He had seventy Apostolic briefs, and if Prince Frederick would hand me over to him as the Pope requested by means of the Rose, he was to nail up one in each city, and so ensure that he would be unmolested as he took me to Rome. But he betrayed his hidden intentions towards me when he said, 'Martin, I thought you were some aged theologian who'd been arguing with himself behind the stove. But I see you are still young and strong. If I had 25,000 armed men I don't believe I could take you to Rome, for I have sounded the feelings of the people all along the way, to find out what they thought about you, and for every one who stands for the Pope there are three against him and for you.' Actually this was nonsense: his soundings had included poor little women and girls in the hostelries, asking what *they* thought of the Roman Seat.[1] They knew nothing of this expression and thought he was speaking about kitchen-chairs, and said, 'How can we know what kind of chairs you have in Rome, wooden or stone?'

He asked me, then, to see what I could do to keep the peace; he would do all he could to get the Pope to do the same. I promised without reservation that I would do everything most promptly that would not play false with my conscience. I too was eager and zealous for peace; I had been dragged into these troubles despite myself, and all my moves had been forced. The blame was not mine.

He had, however, summoned John Tetzel of the preaching Order, who was primarily responsible for these tragic events, and had so broken the man's spirit with threatening words from the Pope, that Tetzel, hitherto so fearsome to all and so fearless in his proclamations, began to waste away and finally succumbed to mental sickness. Before he died I learnt what was happening, and comforted him with a kindly letter, bidding him be of good cheer and not to fear the memory of me. It seems that his death was due to his own conscience and the wrath of the Pope.

Karl [von Miltitz], then, and his schemes, were considered futile; but in my opinion if [Albert] of Mainz had from the start, when I admonished him, and still more if the Pope, before he condemned me without a hearing and gave vent to his rage in the Bulls, had adopted

[1] The Latin *sedes* would be translated 'see', but for the sentence which follows.

the same plan as von Miltitz belatedly took up, and had at the outset quenched the outbursts of Tetzel, things would not have grown to such a furore. The entire blame rests with [Albert] of Mainz, who was deluded by his own cleverness and guile, with which he planned to suppress my teachings and keep his hands on the money he had made through Indulgences. But nowadays counsels are taken in vain, and efforts are bent to no effect. The Lord has awakened and stands ready to judge the people. Even if they could slay us, they wouldn't get what they want – indeed they would lose what they have while we live in safety. Several of them, who have not entirely lost their scent, are already sufficiently aware of this.

[Luther proceeds with the passage given above, p. 5, and ends his *Autobiographical Fragment* thus:]

The Indulgence controversy reached this point by 1520 and 1521. Afterwards came the sacramentarian and Anabaptist controversies, and if I live long enough I shall write about them in a preface to my other volumes.

Farewell, my reader, in the Lord: pray for the increase of the Word against Satan. He is strong and he is evil, and at this time he rages with fury, because he knows that his time is short and the kingdom of the Pope is in danger. But may God confirm in us what he has performed, and perfect the work he began in us, to his glory. Amen.

Latin in Scheel, 186 et seq.★

BOOKS FOR FURTHER READING

More books about Luther in English have been published in the last ten years than in the previous three hundred, so that almost all the available literature is up to date, and almost all is profitable. R. H. Bainton, *Here I Stand* (1951) is the most read, most readable and illuminating popular account. J. M. Todd, *Martin Luther* (1964) by a Catholic layman, and J. Atkinson, *Martin Luther* (Pelican Books, 1967) show the modern consensus between Catholic and evangelical approaches to the Reformation. A. G. Dickens, *Martin Luther and the Reformation* (1967) sets Luther against the background of modern research and in his historical context. R. H. Fife, *The Revolt of Martin Luther* (Columbia University, 1957) is a full-scale study of the young Luther, for those who wish to study his formative years in depth. A brief introduction to this phase is E. G. Rupp, *Luther's Progress to the Diet of Worms* (1951). Introductions to Luther's theology are P. S. Watson, *Let God be God* (1947) and E. G. Rupp, *The Righteousness of God* (1953). Those whose appetites have been whetted by our selections from Luther's letters will find excellent material in *Luther: Letters of Spiritual Counsel* (edited by T. G. Tappert, (Library of Christian Classics, xviii, 1955). The evidence concerning Luther's illnesses is satisfactorily assembled only in a work in German by the Danish Catholic doctor Paul J. Reiter, *Martin Luthers Umwelt, Charakter und Psychose* (ii, Copenhagen, 1941). The Victorian novel by Mrs Rundle Charles, *Chronicles of the Schönberg-Cotta Family*, now reprinted in paperback, has an authentic flavour.